A GLIMPSE

of

WORLD MISSIONS

An Evangelical View

By CLYDE W. TAYLOR

MOODY PRESS

CHICAGO

Printed in the United States of America

A GLIMPSE

of

WORLD MISSIONS

CONTENTS

FOREWORD

OFTEN WE HAVE WISHED for such a volume as this to recommend to friends who wanted a brief survey of missions. It is not easy to produce a reasonably accurate miniature of the world missionary picture.

Here we have a bird's-eye view of world missions that is comprehensive, well-balanced and generally accurate. Dr. Taylor has himself visited many of the fields of which he writes. Besides, he has had personal touch with many of the problems missions face. He has avoided the two dangers that plague most brief treatments of a vast theme: vague generalizations, and the highlighting of some of the less important facts which the author knows best.

Dr. Taylor calls his book, *An Evangelical View*. Certainly evangelicals will find it most interesting and enlightening.

HAROLD R. COOK

"Clyde Taylor is the best equipped author to write a book such as *A Glimpse of World Missions*."

HAROLD J. OCKENGA,
Pastor, Park Street Church, Boston

7

INTRODUCTION

Is it possible to present briefly a comprehensive picture of World Evangelism in our day? This small volume is an attempt to give such a general picture of the progress made in reaching the world for Christ. Also we will try to indicate the most important areas of need. No effort will be made to give a history of missions nor will political, social and economic conditions receive attention except as they relate directly to our world task.

Attention will be focused primarily on those countries known as mission fields, with the exception of Europe where some consideration will be given to the Protestant and Catholic countries.

For the convenience of the reader and those who are accustomed to studying the world by "areas," we are dividing the book into chapters covering the major mission areas: Europe, Africa, Middle East, South Asia, Southeast Asia, Far East, Indonesia and Pacific Islands, and Latin America. No effort will be made to give complete data on lands under Communist control and they will be omitted from statistical tables.

We recognize the impossibility of complete accuracy in giving world statistics. However, by personal observation and the competent help of research assistants, we have endeavored to be as accurate as possible. A bibliography of source materials is appended.

Some terminology may be unfamiliar to the reader and should be defined. We usually think of converts on the mission fields in two categories: those who are baptized members of the church; and those who profess to be Christians, attend the meetings, etc., but have not been baptized. The former we call "church members" or "communicants," and the latter, "Christian community" or "Christian constituency."

When calculating the ratio of Christian workers to population we combine missionaries and national workers to get a more accurate picture. Usually the custom has been to give a ratio of missionary to population.

The reader must bear in mind that this report is written from the evangelical or conservative Protestant viewpoint. As is indicated, there are differences of motive and concept between the older missions and churches that are "ecumenical" in their view, with less stress on theology and more on social and economic factors, and the newer missions and churches that give primary emphasis to Biblical doctrines, evangelism, and reaching the "uttermost part" with the Gospel. At times these differences may lead to completely separate organizations on the field and provide little basis for co-operation. On the other hand, this is not a negative matter but a positive one. It is still possible to keep our lines of communication open.

For the most part, with but few exceptions, evangelicals base their fellowship and local co-operation not on organizations and other secondary relationships, but on the new birth in Christ. Thus new lines of fellowship and communication are established as born-again Christians meet on the far battlefields of the world and co-operate for the winning of lost men and women to Christ.

The missionary statistics used in the book are based principally on the *World Christian Handbook—1957,* but some changes have been made where more recent data was available. The population figures are based on the latest releases of the United Nations.

In order to summarize the scope of this task we include here a resumé of world religions (December, 1957). Many of these totals are at best accurate estimates. It is known, however, that the world population increases annually at the rate of approximately 47 million people. The present population of the world, continuing at the present rate of increase, will double in less than fifty years. Although Protestant missions have seen the work in Africa grow by 12 per cent per year for the last five years, and the Far Eastern church grow by 20 per cent per year, the initial number was not large. In contrast, the Communist forces, starting from a handful, have in thirty-five years taken over more than one billion people—and they continue their march.

In view of this, evangelicals have no hope or expectation of winning the whole world to Christianity but they do want to take the Gospel to every nation, tribe and people, that the Lord may call out a people for His name, build His Church— and when it is complete, come again to earth and take it to Himself. This is the hope of the Church.

WORLD RELIGIOUS STATISTICS*

World Population (U.N. Report, April 1959)		2,790,000,000
Under Communism		1,000,000,000
Christian Religions (estimated)		800,000,000
Protestant	245,000,000	
Roman Catholic°°	423,000,000	
Orthodox°° (Greek, Russian, Syrian)	120,000,000	
Coptic°°	10,000,000	
Animist		121,150,000
Buddhist		150,310,000
Hindu		322,337,286
Muslim		420,600,000

WORLD FOREIGN MISSIONS STATISTICS

Population of Open Mission Fields (Non-Protestant Lands)		1,400,000,000
Christians (approx.) in Open Mission Fields		40,000,000
Foreign Missionaries (Dec. 1957)		38,327
National Workers (Dec. 1957)		154,679
Ratios: Christians to Population	1 to 35	
Workers to Population°°°	1 to 7,254	

MAJORITY OR PREDOMINANT RELIGIONS

Animism	121,150,000
Buddhism	150,310,000
Catholicism, Roman	423,000,000
Catholicism, Eastern	129,192,755
Communism	900,000,000
Hinduism	322,337,286
Islam	420,606,698
Protestantism	245,000,000

*World statistics, even from the best and latest sources, are at best good estimates.
**These count membership from birth regardless of their actual relationship with their church. The Russian Orthodox Church is already included under Communism. Most statistics of non-Christian religions also count children in their totals.
***Workers as used here include both foreign and national workers.

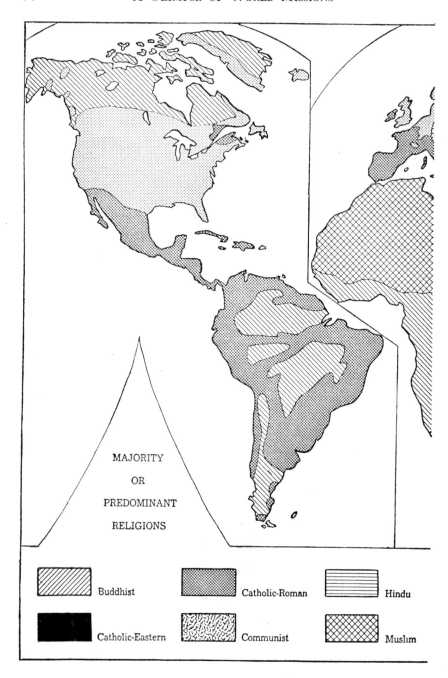

MAJORITY

OR

PREDOMINANT

RELIGIONS

Buddhist   Catholic-Roman   Hindu

Catholic-Eastern   Communist   Muslim

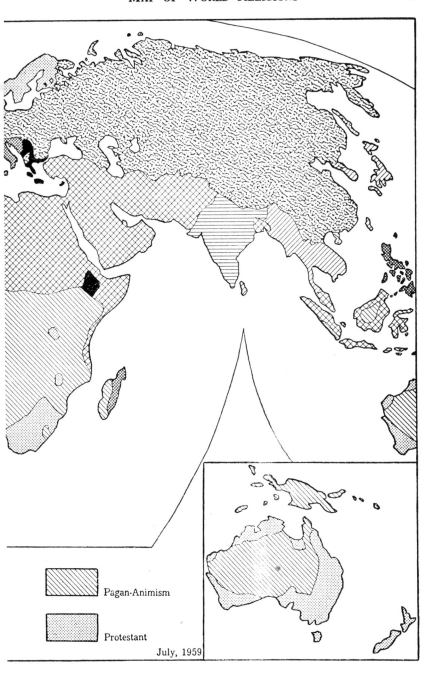

Pagan-Animism

Protestant

July, 1959

EUROPE

IN WORLD EVANGELISM we have usually thought of two Europes, Protestant Europe and Catholic Europe. Now we should add a third, Communist Europe. In each case the term refers to a majority religion.

PROTESTANT EUROPE

The eight countries comprising this group (Switzerland, British Isles including Northern Ireland, Netherlands, West Germany, Denmark, Norway, Sweden, Finland) have much in common. All have Protestant majorities. In most of these countries the state-supported church (Anglican in the British Isles, Reformed in the Netherlands, and Switzerland [Reformed] Lutheran in the rest) has a tendency to take the people as members by birth. This would not be quite as true in England and the Netherlands as in the Lutheran countries. In most of these countries where church lists are kept, only 25 per cent of the people are listed. Active church membership will run from 1 to 6 per cent of the total population. Thus a great open field of evangelism prevails.

In each of these lands religious freedom in the full sense prevails. There are minority religious groups. In West Germany about 43 per cent are Roman Catholic and 52 per cent Protestant. About 41 per cent of Switzerland's population is Roman Catholic. Each country has the so-called "Free Churches" including Baptists, Methodists, Full Gospel, etc.

In general, the Free Church groups or small segments of the state churches provide the missionary vision. They are the sending agencies.

Foreign missionaries entering these countries to assist in evangelism will not be heartily welcomed by Protestant leaders unless they are there at the invitation of the church. Some missionaries work among refugees from Communist lands and co-operate with existing churches. Others have concentrated on special ministries such as Bible institutes, youth or child evangelism, and special evangelistic campaigns. Most Protestant missionaries in Europe are from strongly evangelical missions.

PROTESTANT EUROPE

Country	Population	Density Per Sq. Mile	Religion		Protestant Constituency
Great Britain	51,172,000	543.0	Protestant		46,172,000
Holland	11,009,000	877.8	Protestant	44.3%	4,876,987
(Netherlands)			Roman Catholic	35.8%	
			Jewish	0.2%	
			Others	17 %	
Scandinavia					
Denmark	4,475,000	270.0	Protestant	98 %	4,375,500
Finland	4,333,000	33.2	Protestant	97 %	4,203,010
			Greek Orthodox	2 %	
			Others	1 %	
Norway	3,496,000	27.7	Protestant	96.8%	3,384,128
			Others	3.2%	
Sweden	7,369,000	42.3	Protestant	99 %	7,295,310
			Others	1 %	
Switzerland	5,117,000	318.3	Protestant	57 %	2,916,690
			Roman Catholic	41 %	
			Jewish	.4%	
			Others	1.6%	
West Germany	51,469,000	534.2	Protestant	52.2%	26,866,818
			Roman Catholic	43.8%	
			Others	4.0%	
Totals	138,440,000				100,090,443

CATHOLIC EUROPE

In this we include both Roman and Orthodox Catholics. In the former bloc are Belgium, France, Spain, Portugal, Italy, parts of Switzerland and Austria.

A close study of these lands reveals great variety in the influence of the Roman Church and the attitude of the people. Also we have variety in government, from the dictatorships of Spain and Portugal to the free governments of Italy and France. In some the "anticlericals" (those who oppose the Roman clergy) and the agnostics are dominant. In France approximately 65 per cent of the men are agnostics. Liberalism is prevalent among the French Roman priests. Anticlericalism is strong in Italy. In these countries perhaps as few as 5 to 10 per cent of the people are active in the Roman Church.

In Spain and Portugal there is a concordat between the dictatorships and the Vatican. Thus there is an outward show of strength by the Roman Church. Actually, a huge majority of the people are inactive in the church. Churches are many but empty. The average man on the street is either indifferent to the church or strongly anticlerical. Most church interest is manifested by the women.

By virtue of the concordat, however, all religious education is church controlled. In Spain non-Roman Catholic religions are excluded from the field of education and from public manifestation. Meetings in private homes are illegal. Protestants may not proselyte, print literature, run schools or seminaries, nor hold church services unless the chapel is licensed. Every possible discrimination is made against them. There is much less opposition in Portugal, the greatest problem being the procurement of residence visas for missionaries.

In these countries the results of evangelism are excellent,

A great majority of existing churches are evangelical and evangelistic. Government restrictions are the only drawback.

Since World War II, Italy has seen a great response. The Pentecostal or Full Gospel groups have made the greatest gains. It is difficult to find even a small town in Italy without its halls or meeting places. At present our greatest problem is residence visas for missionaries to Italy. Roman Catholic emphasis in Italy is mostly political, with some effort to halt the march of Protestantism across the country.

CATHOLIC EUROPE

Country	Population	Density Per Sq. Mile	Religion		Protestant Constituency
Austria	6,918,959	215.9	Roman Catholic	89 %	
			Protestant	6 %	415,137
			Others	5 %	
Belgium	6,983,000	215.7	Roman Catholic	89 %	
			Protestant	6 %	418,980
			Others	5 %	
Cyprus	536,000	145.0	Greek Christian	80 %	
France	44,000,000	205.8	Roman Catholic	97.5%	
			Protest. & Others	2.5%	1,100,000
Greece	8,031,000	156.9	Greek Orthodox	96 %	
			Muslim	2 %	
			Jewish	1.1%	
			Others	.9%	7,200
Ireland	2,885,000	108.8	Roman Catholic	94.3%	
			Protestant	5 %	144,250
			Protest. & Others	.7%	
Italy	48,353,000	415.5	Roman Catholic	99.6%	
			Protest. & Others	.4%	200,000
Luxemburg	312,500	312.9	Roman Catholic		
Portugal	8,909,000	249.9	Roman Catholic		12,411
Spain	29,431,000	149.4	Roman Catholic		25,365
Totals	156,359,459				2,323,343

France is unique in its liberalism in both politics and religion. The Roman Church is spiritually ineffective. The people are largely indifferent to religion. Even the Protestant minority (mostly Reformed) has little vision of evangelism. The result is a total of approximately 36,000 towns, cities and villages in France without a Gospel witness. This great need has aroused the interest of foreign missionaries, who, generally speaking, are not welcomed by the national Protestant Church. In many cases the churches have used the services of foreign missionaries, but generally they have shown more interest in financial assistance and have done their own evangelism. The weakness is that only a small fraction of the existing church has any evangelistic vision. Recent campaigns sparked by foreign evangelists have started an awakening in the existing church.

Thus opposition to evangelism varies, from countries like France where it is almost nil, to Spain where every possible obstacle is raised by the Roman Church leaders and enforced by the government.

With the Russian Church dominated by the Communists, the Greek Catholics form the main body of European Orthodox Catholics. In Greece about 96 per cent of the people are listed as Greek Orthodox, with less than 1 per cent being Protestant. However, the Protestant minority is active and evangelistic. The Greek Church is a state religion with full guarantees and support. The net result is a stagnated church that has never been reformed. There are indications that movements within the church may succeed in getting a better educated clergy, with more spiritual life. A lay movement within the Greek Church is encouraging the reading of the New Testament and a revival in the church. The same group, however, persecutes the Protestant minority. While Protestants enjoy constitutional freedom, they suffer local opposition by the orthodox clergy.

The work of the Protestant Church is handicapped by the lack of a good seminary to train workers. Foreign missionaries are not readily received by the Greek Protestants. They believe they are capable of evangelizing the nation but need financial assistance. Several mission agencies .help support Greek workers, and others have entered with a literature program and some evangelistic efforts.

COMMUNIST EUROPE

The reader will have observed that we look upon Communism as a substitute religion. In its march across Europe it has taken over Roman and Orthodox Catholic countries. No Protestant country (except East Germany which was handed over to the Communists by the Allies) has succumbed to Communism. The same religious conditions prevailed in 1941 as now prevail in Catholic Free Europe, with the churches wealthy, decadent and involved in politics. The one exception in Communist Europe was the country of Albania, which was Muslim but is now Communist dominated.

Communism as a religion has many religious terms. It offers redemption (by science) ; it demands consecration and dedication; it has confirmation services for youth; it promotes worship of its leaders; and thus presents itself as a substitute for true religion. Hence the religions behind the Iron Curtain have largely been taken over by the state. The exceptions are those minority groups—Protestants—that have been allowed to retain some church buildings. In them the Christians assemble, report additions each year, but are greatly restricted. They have no youth work and may not openly proselytize. Without a doubt, however, many thousands have remained true to their Lord. Missionary work is prohibited. Our help must be by radio and other means of communication.

AFRICA[1]

THIS GREAT AREA has only one unifying factor—geographic. In every other way, every diversity is found. With some of the world's oldest civilizations, it still has primitive tribes. Seventy-five years ago, pioneers were still driving toward the heart of Africa. When modern missionaries entered Africa there were but 5 written languages. Now there are over 400. While most coastal peoples have been contacted with the Gospel, in some interior areas unreached tribes remain. In general, the Protestant Church in Africa is about twenty-five years behind the Asian in development. At the conference of the International Missionary Council held in Ghana in December, 1957, it was noted that usually Asian delegations were composed of three Asians, or two Asians and a missionary, while delegations from Africa had at least one missionary, and frequently two, to one African.

Africa has about 40 per cent of all Protestant foreign missionaries and 50 per cent of all national workers on foreign fields, and about 30 per cent of Protestant Christians in mis-

AFRICA

Population (U.N. 1959—less Egypt)		200,000,000
Church Members		5,040,471
Christian Community		12,515,423
Native Staff		78,332
Foreign Staff		16,765
Ratios: Christians to Population	1 to 15	
Ratios: Workers to Population	1 to 2,103	

[1] In a present-day world of far-reaching and continuing national and political changes, we have given a fairly accurate report in this information.

23

sion lands. During the last five years the Christian community increased by 60 per cent.

A continent so huge must be considered by regions. The commonly used divisions are: North Africa, West Africa, Central Africa, East Africa, and South Africa. We will consider them in that order.

NORTH AFRICA

This "land of the vanished Church" presents the neediest area in all of Africa. Along the northern coast of Africa, stretched across 3,000 miles, lie Morocco, Algeria, Tunisia and Libya, with over 23 million people. Yet in all that area there are but 2,942 Christians and only 274 workers. There is but one worker for over 80,000 people. In Libya there are only 7 missionaries to reach over a million people.

NORTH AFRICA

Country	Population	Church Members	Christian Community
Algeria	9,390,000	577	1,291
Libya	1,100,000	23	53
Morocco			
French	8,563,117	503	1,288
Spanish	1,010,117	22	100
Tunisia	3,735,000	25	210
Tangier (city)	172,300	41	150
Totals	23,970,534	1,191	3,092

NORTH AFRICA—Cont.

	Native Staff	Foreign Staff	Ratio—Christians to Population	Ratio—Workers to Population
Algeria	19	112	1- 7,273	1- 71,679
Libya	..	7	1-20,754	1-157,142
Morocco				
French	4	86	1- 6,648	1- 95,146
Spanish	..	14	1-10,101	1- 72,151
Tunisia	2	30	1-17,785	1-116,718
Tangier (city)	1	44	1- 1,148	1- 3,828
Totals	26	293	1- 7,752	1- 75,142

The tragedy is that this should never have been so. The early Christian Church spread across this area, but it died and the Muslims took over. Now these lands are from 95 to 98 per cent Muslim. The work is slow and tiring, and the workers too few. In spite of much opposition, missionaries can enter. Because their converts are severely persecuted there is a strong possibility of many secret believers.

An excellent medical work is carried on in several areas and the thousands of Muslims treated annually are all given the Gospel. The Bible is in the language of the people and some schools are operated.

Rio de Oro—Canary Islands

Two other fields are associated with North Africa, Rio de Oro, south of Spanish Morocco on the west coast, and the Canary Islands. The former is almost all Muslim, while the Islands are Roman Catholic. The mainland colony is governed from the Islands. We know of no missionary work in Rio de Oro, but on the Islands two missions with a total staff of 7 missionaries witness on both the major islands. Only one permit for a chapel has been given, although many requests have been made to the Spanish government in Madrid. There are several hundred Christians. Restrictions on Protestant missionary work are about the same as in Spain.

WEST AFRICA

This most densely populated section of Africa has been called the "graveyard of the missionary." The hot, humid, tropical coast, where most work started, is badly infested with malaria and other fevers. The higher plateaus of the interior provide a better climate. To the north this gives way to the barren desert. This area includes what have been known as French West Africa and British West Africa with several other colonies and the free state of Liberia.

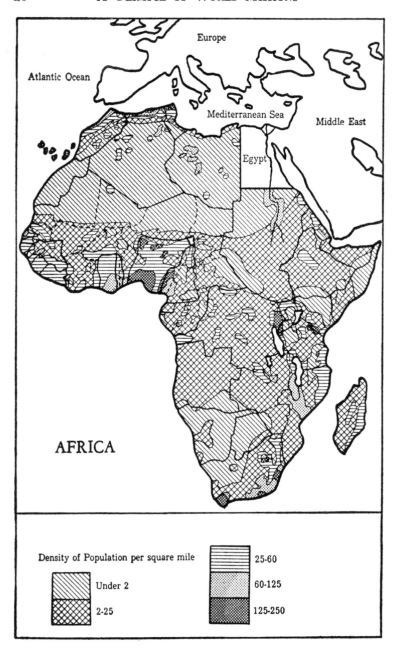

AFRICA

Density of Population per square mile   25-60

Under 2   60-125

2-25   125-250

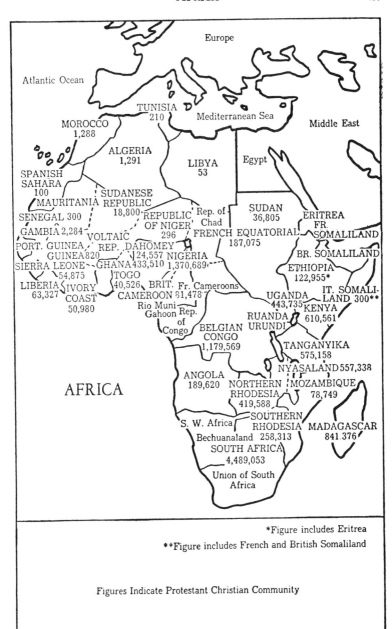

Europe

Atlantic Ocean

TUNISIA
210

Mediterranean Sea

Middle East

MOROCCO
1,288

ALGERIA
1,291

LIBYA
53

Egypt

SPANISH
SAHARA
100

MAURITANIA

SUDANESE
REPUBLIC
18,800

SENEGAL 300

GAMBIA 2,284

PORT. GUINEA
GUINEA 820

SIERRA LEONE
54,875

LIBERIA
63,327

VOLTAIC
REP.

IVORY
COAST
50,980

REPUBLIC
OF NIGER
296

DAHOMEY
24,557

GHANA 433,510

TOGO
40,526

CAMEROON
50,980

Rep. of
Chad

FRENCH EQUATORIAL
187,075

NIGERIA
1,370,689

BRIT.
81,478

Fr. Cameroons

Rio Muni
Gahoon Rep.
of
Congo

BELGIAN
CONGO
1,179,569

SUDAN
36,805

ERITREA

FR.
SOMALILAND

BR. SOMALILAND

ETHIOPIA
122,955*

UGANDA
443,735

RUANDA
URUNDI

IT. SOMALI-
LAND 300**

KENYA
610,561

TANGANYIKA
575,158

AFRICA

ANGOLA
189,620

NORTHERN
RHODESIA
419,588

SOUTHERN
RHODESIA
258,313

NYASALAND 557,338

MOZAMBIQUE
78,749

MADAGASCAR
841,376

S. W. Africa

Bechuanaland

SOUTH AFRICA
4,489,053

Union of South
Africa

*Figure includes Eritrea

**Figure includes French and British Somaliland

Figures Indicate Protestant Christian Community

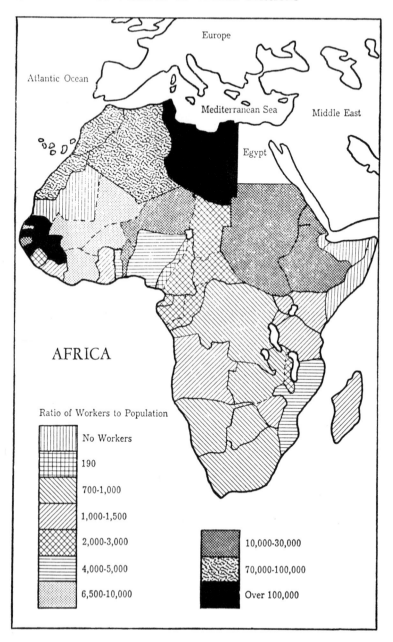

AFRICA

Ratio of Workers to Population

No Workers	
190	
700-1,000	
1,000-1,500	
2,000-3,000	
4,000-5,000	
6,500-10,000	

| 10,000-30,000 |
| 70,000-100,000 |
| Over 100,000 |

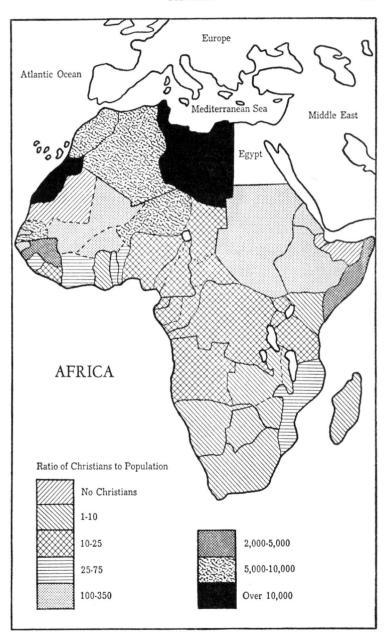

Europe

Atlantic Ocean

Mediterranean Sea

Middle East

Egypt

AFRICA

Ratio of Christians to Population

No Christians

1-10

10-25

25-75

100-350

2,000-5,000

5,000-10,000

Over 10,000

WEST AFRICA

Country	Population	Church Members	Christian Community
British			
Cameroons	1,430,000	45,746	81,478
Gambia	264,000	1,686	2,284
Ghana	5,114,000	145,343	481,510
Nigeria	30,500,000	287,026	1,370,689
Sierra Leone	2,050,000	24,344	54,875
French			
Dahomey	1,620,000	4,543	24,557
Sudanese Republic	3,600,000	6,960	18,800
Guinea	2,340,000	10	820
Ivory Coast	2,240,000	11,149	50,980
Niger	2,280,000	53	296
Senegal	2,220,000	100	300
Togo	1,070,000	8,844	40,526
Liberia	1,250,000	29,980	63,327
Spanish and Portuguese	1,886,441	3,419	5,388
Totals	57,864,441	569,203	2,195,830

WEST AFRICA—*Cont.*

	Native Staff	Foreign Staff	Ratio—Christians to Population	Ratio—Workers to Population
British				
Cameroons	659	98	1- 17	1- 189
Gambia	24	15	1- 111	1- 6,769
Ghana	3,192	238	1- 10	1- 1,487
Nigeria	7,079	2,047	1- 22	1- 3,342
Sierra Leone	538	149	1- 37	1- 2,984
French				
Dahomey	75	39	1- 65	1- 14,210
Sudanese Republic	174	90	1- 191	1- 13,639
Guinea	222	63	1- 2,854	1- 8,140
Ivory Coast	276	87	1- 43	1- 6,170
Niger	37	51	1- 7,702	1- 25,909
Senegal	..	13	1- 7,400	1-170,769
Togo	191	40	1- 26	1- 4,632
Liberia	584	337	1- 19	1- 1,357
Spanish and Portuguese	37	27	1- 350	1- 29,475
Totals	13,088	3,294	1- 26	1- 3,503

The missions working in the area are largely evangelical, many of them having entered during the last twenty-five years. A great effort has been made to reduce the tribal languages to writing, but there are still some 41 tribal languages (not counting dialects) into which the Scriptures have not been translated. Several of these are now being reduced to writing.

Political developments have been most unexpected in this area, especially in the French community. Guinea has received its independence. Mauritania, Senegal, Ivory Coast, Niger, French Sudan, Upper Volta, Togo and Dahomey have remained in the French community with much autonomy. All, however, have remained open to the Gospel with continuing freedom to evangelize. In all, the Muslims have made great advances so that some areas are almost completely Muslim, such as Mauritania, Niger, and large sections of Guinea, and French Sudan. Some tribes have completely resisted Islam and its teachers. Many tribes retain their fetishism, even some that outwardly embrace Islam.

Mauritania, with over 600,000 people, almost totally Moslim, is completely neglected although some missions work on its southern and eastern borders. It is a huge area sparsely populated. Next in need is Senegal. For many years one European mission had sole occupancy of this entire area. Recently several others have entered on the east. The city of Dakar has been greatly neglected. Apart from these there are mission agencies in all other general areas. The need is for personnel to close in the gaps. Many of these are small tribes that have been by-passed. Now the linguistic task confronts us.

British West Africa includes Gambia, Sierra Leone, Ghana, British Togo and British Cameroons, and Nigeria. The first is a very small Crown colony just below Senegal. Two English societies still carry on a limited work there. The schools have been taken over by the government.

Sierra Leone, one of the oldest British colonies and still quite backward, is well occupied with missions, most of which are thoroughly evangelical. There is still much to be done, but it can be done within the framework of the existing missions.

Ghana, the new republic, continues to offer complete freedom to preach the Gospel. In fact, it uses a Christian hymn as its national anthem. However, the concentration of Christians is in the south. The work in the north is newer with much territory to be reached. Several strong evangelical missions have entered here and are pushing ahead with evangelization.

Nigeria is the brightest spot in West Africa for the Gospel. Although strongly Muslim in the north (Muslims entered in the eighth century) there has been a good response among them, with the bulk of the Christians coming from the pagan tribes of the south. Nigeria has over 9,000 workers and missionaries with strong churches in many areas. It is one of the best occupied fields in Africa.

British Cameroons—This portion of the Cameroons, once a German colony, is a trust or mandated area and is administered by the British along with Nigeria. First reached by British Baptists, the work was later turned over to a German Swiss society and after World War I has been the work of the American German Baptists as their main mission enterprise. The field has been fairly well evangelized.

British Togoland is also a trust territory with about 10 per cent of the population confessed Christians, mostly in the south. The north is a needy field. Recently one evangelical mission has entered.

Portuguese West Africa consists of Portuguese Guinea and three sets of islands, the Azores, Madeiras, and Cape Verde. Portuguese Guinea, mostly Roman Catholic, has but one mission with only 9 missionaries for over a half million people. The work is new. On the islands much of the Gospel witness is through national leaders and pastors. One evangelical mission has a strong work on one of the Cape Verde Islands. All of the islands are primarily Roman Catholic, and it is not easy for foreign missionaries to establish residence. There are less than 10,000 Protestant Christians on all three groups of islands.

Spanish West Africa consists of óne small colony, Spanish Guinea (Rio Muni), and two islands, Fernando Poo and Sao Tome. All of these have been reached with the Gospel, but the Christian community is small. All have been heavily influenced by Roman Catholicism. Some strong national Christian churches have been established.

Liberia is a free republic with complete religious freedom. It has been reached in part by Muslims, but still has a majority of people under fetish worship. It is said to be one of the most demon-possessed countries on earth, especially among the people of the interior. Communications are the big problem, since the coastal region is separated from the interior by an almost impassable swamp extending virtually the entire length of the country. The recently established radio station is helping to reach many of the people. Fifteen mission agencies with over 900 workers are endeavoring to reach the country for Christ. Nine tribes need Scriptures in writing. One tribe of 25,000 is untouched.

CENTRAL AFRICA

This huge heart of Africa has developed under the influence of the French and Belgians—the French area known in

the past as French Equatorial Africa and the Belgian area
known as the Belgian Congo including the mandated territory of Ruanda-Urundi. This great area covers almost 2
million square miles with a population of about 17 millions,
mostly concentrated in the southern sections, with over 12
millions in the Congo. The northern portion is very sparsely
settled. The former French Equatorial Africa is now divided
into four sections called the Republic of Chad, Republic of
Congo, Gabon and the French Cameroons. The French Cameroons is a mandated territory and due to receive its independence soon. In each of these areas there are unreached
tribes and areas, none large and all within areas for which
missions have assumed responsibility. In some cases more
missionaries are needed. There is linguistic work to be done.
In the far south the dense jungles make work difficult. All
types of work are carried on and efforts are made to reach
neglected tribes. In the Gabon, efforts to reach the nomadic
pygmies progress and all major areas are being penetrated.

CENTRAL AFRICA

Country	Population	Church Members	Christian Community
Belgian Congo	16,600,000	654,728	1,179,569
French Equatorial	7,885,600	244,479	513,380
Totals	24,485,600	899,207	1,692,949

CENTRAL AFRICA—Cont.

	Native Staff	Foreign Staff	Ratio—Christians to Population	Ratio—Workers to Population
Belgian Congo	20,269	2,146	1- 14	1- 741
French Equatorial	4,182	830	1- 15	1- 1,573
Totals	24,451	2,976	1- 14	1- 892

In the Cameroons and adjacent areas a strong national
church has developed that should be assuming major responsibilities in evangelism. In the Gabon, and what was known

as the Ubangi-Shari areas, the work is newer and more missionary work needed.

Congo²—In the heart of Africa, largely untouched by Muslims, some 47 mission agencies are systematically trying to reach the 16 million people and build a strong church. In most areas they operate the primary school system and teacher training programs. There are 22,000 workers who already count 10 per cent of the population as confessed Christians. In the Ruanda-Urundi area approximately one-third of the people are Christians. As in many sections of Africa the majority of the work is in the villages. There are no areas of sufficient size to warrant the entrance of a new mission, but there are many small sections that have not been reached.

Here some 15 languages and major dialects have no translation of the Scriptures. There is a great need for secondary schools and seminaries for advanced training of church leaders. Steps are being taken to establish at least two union seminaries, one in the south and one in the north. Evangelical missions, however, are wary of secondary schools and colleges, with the result that the educational picture is not bright for most of the evangelical work in Africa.

EAST AFRICA

Stretching from the southern borders of Egypt to Mozambique we have East Africa, with four British colonies or protectorates, the independent countries of Ethiopia, Sudan and Italian Somaliland. Here we find some of the most beautiful country in all of Africa, especially the plateaus of Tanganyika, Kenya, Uganda and Ethiopia.

Tanganyika, now a United Nations trusteeship of Great Britain, was previously known as German East Africa. Mission work has been carried on here for a century, some of it among

2 Name Belgian Congo retained elsewhere in text for easy reference,

most primitive peoples. British missions came first, then German, and finally American. Several new missions have entered in the last five years. So as far as missions are concerned there are sufficient agencies. There are presently over 5,500 workers to reach 8½ million people. The response has been good, considering that the Muslims are strong along the east coast. Although Tanganyika is not as far advanced politically as Kenya and Uganda, nationalism is strong. Some of the churches are well advanced. Of the almost 600,000 Christians about 275,000 are Lutheran, 175,000 Anglican, and the remainder from other European and American missions. As far as can be determined, almost half of the 137 tribes are without Scriptures and a number have not been touched with the Gospel.

EAST AFRICA

Country	Population	Church Members	Christian Community
Ethiopia and Eritrea	19,500,000	96,066	122,955
Kenya	6,150,000	291,118	610,561
Somalilands	2,049,000	......	300
Sudan	10,209,703	11,799	36,805
Tanganyika	8,250,000	263,702	575,158
Uganda	5,450,000	146,089	443,735
Totals	49,823,203	808,774	1,789,514

EAST AFRICA—Cont.

	Native Staff	Forcign Staff	Ratio—Christians to Population	Ratio—Workers to Population
Ethiopia and Eritrea	675	487	1- 158	1- 16,781
Kenya	4,230	847	1- 10	1- 1,211
Somalilands	..	..	1- 4,212	..
Sudan	653	241	1- 277	1- 11,420
Tanganyika	4,917	672	1- 14	1- 1,476
Uganda	3,917	73	1- 12	1- 1,366
Totals	14,392	2,320	1- 27	1- 2,981

Kenya—Foreigners came to this colony first for financial benefits. Today the white population occupies the best lands of the colony, which was part of the reason for the Mau Mau uprising. The Africans have been pushed into the less desirable areas. In spite of this tension, however, missions have pushed ahead in almost all parts of Kenya and only a few large areas are left without a witness. Protestant missions have assumed much responsibility in operating primary schools, but the government is taking this responsibility as rapidly as possible. Teachers, however, are still being trained by missions.

The most recent survey of tribes indicates that about 13 tribes with a total of 250,000 people have not been reached with the Word. This task, plus that of rapidly building a strong church to keep pace with political developments, is the challenge of the day for Kenya.

Uganda is one of the most interesting of the African fields. It is distinctive for several reasons. A great majority of the people have been reached and there has been an excellent response to the Gospel. Yet, a number of Uganda's 47 separate tribes have not been evangelized. One tribe of 80,000 was just entered in 1958, and two other large tribes need workers and translation work done on the languages.

The other unique factor is that even though Uganda is a country of almost 5½ million people, there are only five mission societies operating in the whole colony. Of these five, by far the larger work has been done by the Church Missionary Society of England, which has carried on a very strong and spiritual work down through the years. Uganda has been blessed by a great revival, but there are still areas that need to be reached by the Gospel of Jesus Christ. Conceivably this could best be done by the evangelical societies already operating in the country.

Sudan—Straddling the Nile just south of Egypt is this new nation of some 10 million people and as large as Alaska, Texas and New Mexico all in one. It is divided roughly into two major sections, the northern portion which is almost totally Muslim, and the southern part which is largely composed of pagan tribes.

Entering the Sudan from the north at the end of the nineteenth century, the first missionaries found the Muslims almost impervious to the Gospel. Thus their work was largely medical and educational, and this tendency has continued until today. More recently other evangelical missions have entered from the south, especially into the pagan tribes. Although the work has been going on for over half a century, with a total staff of almost 800 at present, there are not more than 40,000 professed Christians in both North and South Sudan, with the majority of them being in the South. The government is very largely Muslim and as such is not welcoming an expansion of missionary effort in the country. A number of Catholic missionaries and some Protestant missionaries have been requested to leave.

Ethiopia and Eritrea—We are considering these two areas jointly since they are now politically related, and Eritrea down through the years has been associated with Ethiopia. During this century it has changed hands several times, but now as an autonomous government is federated with Ethiopia.

This area of approximately 20 million people first heard the Gospel in the third century and was very largely evangelized. In spite of wars and conquests it has remained a non-Muslim oasis in the midst of the great Mohammedan masses of North and Northeast Africa. The Coptic Church, however, has very largely obscured the Gospel through superstition and ignorance and has never reached the tribespeople in the south and west of the country.

Today there are some 17 European and American missions in Eritrea and Ethiopia, working mostly with the tribespeople and the non-Coptic people. They are heavily restricted in their ministry among the Copts, because this official religion of Ethiopia is classified as one of the Christian faiths and they do not permit proselytizing. Some of the Christians, however, work among them in an effort to awaken the church itself.

There are some 17 tribal languages into which the Scriptures should be translated and the people reached with the Gospel, but a real problem exists because of the fact that the Ethiopian government has adopted a policy of restricting the use of tribal languages, particularly in the field of literacy and education. This has made it very difficult for the missionaries to present the Scriptures to the people in their own language and has made it equally difficult to teach these people Amharic, the national language of Ethiopia. It is difficult for new missions or missionaries to enter the country, since this must be done by permission of the Crown. Territories are allotted by the Crown and other organizations are not allowed to overlap.

The Somalilands—French, British and Italian Somalilands, strips of land along the Red Sea and Indian Ocean, very nearly isolate Ethiopia from the coast. These coastal areas have for many years been almost solidly Muslim in population. French Somaliland, the smallest of the three, has no Protestant work except for an occasional representative of the Bible Society. The Roman Catholics carry on a work through schools and other institutions, but mostly for the Europeans there. In British Somaliland no missionary work is officially permitted. Mission representatives occasionally enter, but not with official residence. The Bible Societies do make an effort in the distribution of the Scriptures. Italian Somaliland has had a Protestant mission in the past, but when Italy invaded the country the missionaries were driven out and all of their properties were taken over by the Roman

Catholic Church. Since that time this work has largely become a ministry to the Italian immigrants. More recently,
one of the North American missions has entered Somaliland
and it may be possible now for some to be won to Christ.

SOUTH AFRICA

The southern quarter of Africa (those countries south of
10° latitude south) are usually considered as an entity in
world missions. However, this does not imply uniformity.
In the Union of South Africa we find modern civilization
and modern cities. A few hundred miles away live Africans
little touched by modern civilization. The one thing in common is the high degree of penetration by the Gospel through
most of this region. Yet even here, one large area (North
Mozambique) is virtually untouched.

SOUTH AFRICA

Country	Population	Church Members	Christian Community
Angola	4,260,000	81,622	189,620
Madagascar	4,450,000	194,615	841,376
Mozambique	6,000,000	39,843	78,749
Nyasaland	2,510,000	213,942	557,338
Rhodesia			
North	2,100,000	68,563	419,588
South	2,360,000	138,643	258,313
Union of South Africa	14,418,000	2,024,868	4,489,053
Totals	36,098,000	2,762,096	6,834,038

SOUTH AFRICA—Cont.

	Native Staff	Foreign Staff	Ratio—Christians to Population	Ratio—Workers to Population
Angola	3,788	328	1- 22	1- 1,035
Madagascar	3,587	112	1- 5	1- 1,203
Mozambique	1,262	240	1- 76	1- 3,995
Nyasaland	874	231	1- 4	1- 2,271
Rhodesia				
North	1,815	710	1- 5	1- 831
South	1,581	631	1- 9	1- 1,066
Union of South Africa	13,682	5,628	1- 3	1- 741
Totals	26,589	7,880	1- 5	1- 1,047

In South Africa we group the countries as follows: Union of South Africa, the Federation of Southern and Northern Rhodesia and Nyasaland, Portuguese Southwest Africa (Angola), Portuguese Southeast Africa (Mozambique), and the French island of Madagascar.

Union of South Africa (Swaziland, Basutoland, Bechuanaland, Southwest Africa). This area is difficult to evaluate as a mission field, for the Union is largely a Protestant land with a large European population and has strong Reformed, Lutheran, Anglican, Methodist, Baptist, and Presbyterian churches, in addition to large Pentecostal denominations. Often these churches have a majority of European members. The 82 recognized Protestant organizations (not counting 1,100 African "Christian" sects) have a total community of about 4½ millions of whom at least 2½ millions are Africans. One-third of all foreign workers and one-sixth of all national workers in Africa are located in this area.

There are two great areas of need— (1) to thoroughly reach the cities with hundreds of thousands living in new African settlements, and (2) to fill in the gaps out in the native areas.

The Bantu Education Act in South Africa placed the primary (and later secondary) schools under government control, thus releasing many missionaries to evangelism and other ministries. The field is wide open, and there is a great response among the Africans. Given a revival in the African church the area should become self-evangelizing.

Many of the nondenominational evangelical missions have offices and sending boards in South Africa, and some of the denominations have their mission boards sending missionaries to other parts of Africa and all over the world. The general impression received is that the Protestant denominations have little vision of home missions.

In this section of Africa 1,100 so-called "Christian" sects

have sprung up. Some of them have thousands of members. Most of them emphasize one aspect of Christian teaching and build their organization around it, or around an outstanding leader.

In implementing its *apartheid* policies the present government has complicated the work of Christian missions, as it demands segregation of races (including residence and assemblage) with division between: white, African (Negro), colored (mulatto), and Indian. This has necessitated the multiplication of churches, theological schools and other institutions.

Central Africa Federation (Northern and Southern Rhodesia and Nyasaland)—These three countries (the first two colonies and the latter a protectorate of Great Britain) have been organized into a federation with the hope of giving it freedom as a dominion in the British Commonwealth. Politically the situation is serious. Violence has been stirred up, mostly in Nyasaland where the white population is small. The dominance of the white minority (although large in Southern Rhodesia and considerable in Northern Rhodesia) has complicated the work of foreign missionaries in these countries. In Nyasaland violence has made it necessary for several missionaries to flee, even though they were not involved in the political tensions.

Of the 6,970,000 population, almost equally divided between the three countries, about 15 per cent are professed Christians and there is one worker for approximately every 1,200 people. The response, however, has been much greater in Nyasaland. The fewer the Europeans, the greater the response.

Missionaries entered the area at the end of the nineteenth century and have now occupied the major areas with some minor areas remaining to be reached. The great need now is for a mature church, and well-trained church leaders to assume the task of evangelism in an area which is likely to see reduction of missionary staff if political tensions increase. With 36 missions having a total of 1,572 foreign missionaries, the need is fairly well met.

Portuguese Southwest Africa (Angola) —The Portuguese colonies in Africa are consistently among those least evangelized. Part of this is due to the effective work of the Roman Church in hindering the entrance of Protestant missionaries. In other instances, it is true that their colonies are less developed. In Angola, out of 4 million people there are less than 200,000 Christians, yet there are over 4,000 workers. This speaks well for the preparation of workers by existing missions, and in general indicates a good response to the message. There are still unreached areas, but it is difficult to secure residence visas for new missionaries to this colony. Without a doubt, there is a great need for revival in the church with a new vision or propagation of the Gospel by the national church. A majority of the missionaries are from the older denominational missions, three of which are from the United States.

Portuguese Southeast Africa (Mozambique) —This colony has presented one of the closed doors to foreign missions since the northern part was closed to missionaries. Missions have been active in the southern half for many years, although many obstacles arose. The climate is very bad and has greatly hampered the work. Roman Catholicism has been dominant for 350 years with considerable control over the government. The Muslims have also come down the coast and won many converts.

Where the Gospel has been presented the response has

been very good. However, much of the work (especially in western Mozambique) has been raised up by native evangelists and Christians who entered from the Rhodesias. Several missions have been started in this way. There are now some churches in the north, but missionary work is still quite restricted. Moreover, as a Portuguese colony it is difficult to get residence visas for Protestant missionaries. Several years ago the Roman Catholic archbishop called for the elimination of Protestants, Muslim and Communists from all of Mozambique. This same influence has made it difficult to get recognized teachers for our Protestant schools. To be recognized the teacher must graduate from a state school, but these only accept Roman Catholic students.

Madagascar—This French territory has a background of African, Arab and Malagasy culture, which had produced a vicious and depraved society by the time the missionaries arrived. The island has had a violent history extending into this century. Here the golden opportunity of missions came a hundred years ago. After much persecution and renewal of pagan rites on the island the church today is maturing, with some 850,000 constituents and 3,600 workers. The missionary staff is reduced, with the church assuming the responsibility of the work. In general the church is not evangelistic in its emphasis.

Resumé for the continent of Africa

In addition to the great spiritual needs of the church in Africa, the following would seem to be the greatest needs of the continent.

1. Africa has been noted for its mission work in the villages and rural areas. Today attention must be given to the needs of the greatly expanding cities that are frequently neglected.

2. Definite plans should be undertaken by all missions contiguous to unreached tribes, to complete the linguistic task and give the people the Scriptures in their own language, at the same time making an effort to reach them with the Gospel. There are probably over 400 tribes in Africa that still have nothing of the Scriptures in their own language. A very large percentage of these tribes, many of which are small, have never been reached with the Gospel.

3. A much greater effort must be made by missions to challenge of the church in Africa with its responsibilities of leadership and propagation of the Gospel. It should be possible in many areas for mission stations as such to be closed, leaving the work completely invested in the hands of the African church. This would release missionary personnel for the final advance into unreached areas.

4. Since in Africa, more than in any other continent, the mission societies have assumed responsibility in the field of primary education, it is most important that this work should not receive undue emphasis. In most cases, in fact, it would be advantageous to hand this work over to the government when possible and give more consideration to higher education, particularly the establishment of secondary schools, colleges, and more seminaries for the preparation of leadership.

5. Although many prophets foretell the closing of Africa, there is at present little indication that an antimissionary move will result from the efforts of the nationalist movements to gain independence for their respective countries. It has not turned out that way in those nations which thus far have succeeded in getting their independence.

THE MIDDLE EAST

THIS AREA, the cradle of three of the world's great religions, Judaism, Christianity and Islam, has like North Africa been most difficult to reach for the Gospel. This has not been due particularly to lack of missionary interest, but to the fact that the countries (with the exception of Israel) are all dominated by the Muslim faith. In Most of the countries it is actually illegal for a person to change his religious belief, and where it is permissible it entails re-registering with the government under a new religion, because registration includes religion. It may also include the changing of the convert's name. Religious persecution, of course, is taken for granted under these circumstances.

This great area includes the following countries: United Arab Republic (which includes both Egypt and Syria) , Lebanon, Turkey, Iraq, Iran, Jordan, Afghanistan, Saudi Arabia, Yemen, Aden, Oman, and Israel.

It should be noted that although there are almost 100 million people in this area, the total Christian community is only about 200,000. Thus there is approximately one Christian to each 500 population. Here after one hundred years of missionary work the total number of workers is only about 2,536. This makes one Christian worker to approximately 40,000 people.

MIDDLE EAST

Country	Population	Church Members	Christian Community
Arabia and Aden	13,423,441	372	729
Egypt	24,410,000	40,148	116,227
Iran	21,794,000	4,512	9,005
Iraq	6,538,000	676	1,629
Israel	1,924,000	1,295	1,536
Jordan	1,527,000	2,789	5,802
Lebanon and Syria	1,525,000 3,970,000	13,293	57,530
Turkey	24,797,000	67	5,213
Totals	99,908,441	63,152	197,671

MIDDLE EAST—Cont.

	Native Staff	Foreign Staff	Ratio—Christians to Population	Ratio—Workers to Population
Arabia and Aden	58	88	1-18,413	1- 91,941
Egypt	997	100	1- 210	1- 22,255
Iran	109	134	1- 2,420	1- 89,687
Iraq	7	18	1- 4,013	1-261,520
Israel	53	130	1- 1,253	1- 10,513
Jordan	54	61	1- 26	1- 13,278
Lebanon and Syria	330	168	1- 96	1- 11,034
Turkey	..	50	1- 4,757	1-495,940
Totals	1,608	749	1- 590	1- 42,387

UNITED ARAB REPUBLIC

This republic, recently organized as a union of Egypt and Syria, is an initial step in an effort to unite all the Arab nations together into one large republic. Initiated by Egypt, it has thus far succeeded only in getting complete union of these two countries. However, mission-wise, we will have to consider them as separate entities.

Egypt—This country, so often appearing in Biblical accounts, has the second largest population of all the Middle Eastern countries. An early recipient of Christianity, it is now one of the great centers of the Muslim faith, where one of the largest Muslim universities is located, and from which thou-

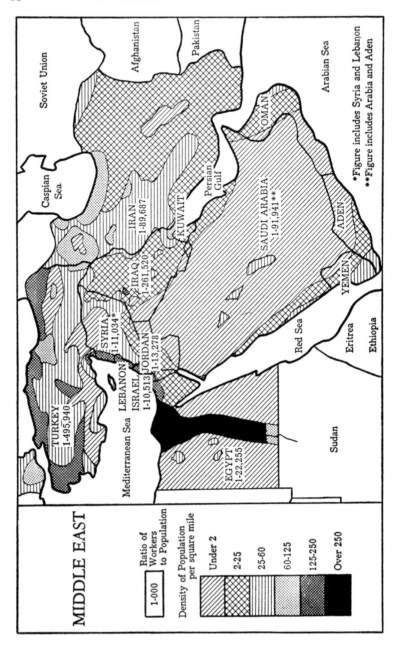

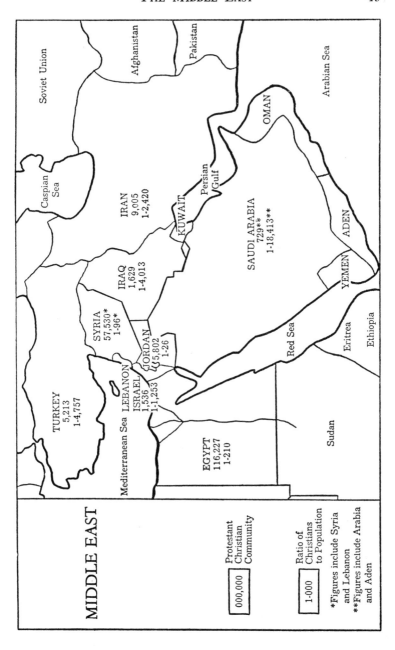

MIDDLE EAST

Soviet Union

Afghanistan

Pakistan

Arabian Sea

Caspian
Sea

OMAN

Persian
Gulf

IRAN
9,005
1-2,420

KUWAIT

SAUDI ARABIA
729**
1-18,413**

ADEN

IRAQ
1,629
1-4,013

YEMEN

SYRIA
57,530*
1-96*

JORDAN
5,802
1-26

Red Sea

Eritrea

Ethiopia

TURKEY
5,213
1-4,757

Mediterranean Sea LEBANON

ISRAEL
1,536
1-1,253

EGYPT
116,227
1-210

Sudan

000,000 Protestant
         Christian
         Community

1-000   Ratio of
        Christians
        to Population

*Figures include Syria
 and Lebanon
**Figures include Arabia
 and Aden

sands of Muslim missionaries have been sent to convert the Africans. Since for many years Egypt was under British control there was complete religious freedom, and this freedom still exists to a large degree. Missionaries have preached the Gospel the length and breadth of the land. However, they are prohibited legally from proselytizing Muslims, so most of their results have come in the form of converts from the Coptic Church. Some 20 Protestant missionary agencies have worked in Egypt, many of these being British, up until the time of the Suez trouble when they were expelled. A few have returned. There is, however, a strong national church in Egypt that is carrying on an effective work assisted by American and other missionaries. A large number of schools and hospitals are operating, and most encouraging is a lay movement in Egypt among the churches themselves to promote soul winning throughout the country. The literature work, which was in Cairo, has been transferred to Lebanon because of the recent troubles in Egypt. The total Christian community in all of Egypt is about 116,000, with approximately 1,000 national workers and 100 missionaries.

Syria—Syria and Lebanon have frequently been grouped together in missionary surveys and reports, probably because of the fact that these were under French control for a number of years. During that period both were open and most of the missionaries, of course, entered through Lebanon.

Since both these nations have received their independence, they must now be considered as separate missionary entities. Under the present regime virtually all the missionaries have been requested to leave Syria, so that at the present time the church that continues is directed and led entirely by its national leaders. Much of the strength of Syria has been found among the Armenian groups, especially in North Syria. Also

there have been a number of converts from the Syrian Orthodox Church and other non-Muslim groups. Much of the
work in this area has centered around schools, clinics, and
hospitals in an endeavor to reach the Muslims for Christ.

Because many of these Christians have emigrated from Syria
to South America and other areas, the actual size of the church
has diminished. At the present time there are less than
60,000 Protestant Christians in all of Syria and Lebanon.
Many of the missionaries leaving Syria have moved over into
Lebanon and are currently working there.

Lebanon—This little republic on the Mediterranean coast,
once a part of Turkey, maintains a delicate balance of power
between members of the Eastern Orthodox Church and Muslims. Each claims approximately 50 per cent of the population. Protestant Christians are a small minority. However,
there is complete religious freedom, and Lebanon has been
rather generous in granting residence visas. Currently this
little country of about 1½ million population has a very high
birth rate (seven times the death rate), which means a rapidly increasing population. There are a very large number
of Bible training schools for training nationals, several colleges and a seminary, with every type of Christian work being
carried on in the little republic. The literature work of
Egypt has been transferred to Beirut, so that actually there
is a large missionary personnel in proportion to the population in Lebanon. Here, as in all of the Middle East, the
greater response of converts is from those who are members
of the ancient Eastern Orthodox churches, but a good number of Muslims are also being reached.

Turkey, Iraq, Iran and Jordan may be considered as a group
because of their similar circumstances and conditions. Although Islam is the official religion of these four coun-

tries, freedom of religion exists in all of them. Protestant work has been carried on for many years but the results have been very meager, with most of the converts coming from the non-Muslim minorities, or through the establishment of orphanages and schools training children in the Protestant faith.

There are about 20,000 professed Christians in all four of these countries put together, and the number of missionaries is relatively high considering the small Christian community. However, this is always expected in Muslim countries. The recent political disturbances in the area have reduced the missionary population, particularly in Iraq, and the future of missions in these areas is precarious. Those Christians who have taken their stand have endured the trial of their faith but in many cases the church is so small that it is not even organized.

Many areas of these countries, including small villages and nomadic groups, have never heard the Gospel.

Afghanistan—This kingdom, an independent constitutional monarchy, is a Muslim state. It is entirely closed to missionary work. There is a small Christian church in the capital to care for the needs of the foreign Christian community. Most missionary work that has been carried on with Afghans has been carried on at the Afghan border. Converts are too few to be listed.

Arabia—In Saudi Arabia we also include the countries of Yemen, Aden, and Oman. These are all small areas except Saudi Arabia, and it is largely a barren desert. This is the very heart of the Mohammedan empire, and Islam is strongest here.

Missionary work has been carried on for a number of years. Frequently missionaries have outnumbered national

Christians by two or three to one. At the present time there are not over 200 Christians in all of these countries, with the exception of Aden, a British protectorate, where there is freedom of religion and where there has been a slightly larger response to the Gospel. There are over a thousand miles of coast line without a single missionary and most areas have no Christian witness at all. There is little legal provision made for a Muslim to change his faith. There is no organized indigenous church in Saudi Arabia, and the most effective way of making friends has been by means of a medical ministry.

Israel—This homeland of many hundreds of thousands of refugees is also a mission field and has been the object of interest of practically every Jewish missionary society in the world. It is one of the most difficult countries to evaluate, as far as the progress of missions is concerned. Currently the population is approaching the 2 million mark. In all of the country there are only about 1,300 Protestant church members, an overwhelming majority of these being Arab Christians. There are very few Jewish Christians in Israel. The last available statistics indicated that there were 130 missionaries and 53 national workers in Israel for a total church membership of approximately 1,300; or, looking at it in another way, approximately one worker for every seven professed Christians. However, it is very difficult to get accurate statistics because a number of the agencies do not report, and there are without doubt many secret believers in Israel. The Israeli government is not granting residence visas as it once did, and there is considerable persecution of converts by extreme Jewish sects.

SOUTH ASIA

THIS SUBCONTINENT OF ASIA, comprising East and West Pakistan, India, Burma and Ceylon, has a total population in excess of 500 million and today offers the largest solid bloc of people available to the Gospel anywhere. All of these countries are open to the Gospel, although there are restrictions on entrance of missionaries in one or two areas.

Although there are many similarities in the problems and aspects of the work, yet it would be best to consider these four areas, including also the small countries of Nepal and Bhutan, separately.

SOUTH ASIA

Country	Population	Church Members	Christian Community
Burma	20,054,000	224,878	506,131
India	392,440,000	1,750,000	5,999,561
Ceylon	8,929,000	60,540	203,944
Nepal	8,431,537	. . . . . .	. . . . . .
Pakistan	84,777,000	111,636	272,166
Totals	514,631,537	2,147,054	6,981,802

SOUTH ASIA—Cont.

	Native Staff	Foreign Staff	Ratio—Christians to Population	Ratio—Workers to Population
Burma	1,877	150	1- 39	1- 9,893
India	25,173	4,844	1- 65	1- 13,073
Ceylon	830	208	1- 43	1- 8,602
Nepal	32	28	. .	1-140,525
Pakistan	689	700	1- 311	1- 61,034
Totals	28,602	5,930	1- 74	1- 15,100

PAKISTAN

This relatively new country divided into two sections over 1,000 miles apart, known as West Pakistan and East Pakistan, is about 83 per cent Muslim, 13 per cent Hindu, and 4 per cent others (largely Christian). This new nation, a member of the British Commonwealth, offers complete religious freedom in spite of being a Muslim state. The Muslim forces are not united but are divided up into four or five powerful sects that compete with and oppose each other. The government has been remarkably stable considering the turmoil out of which it was born. It, like all new nations, has had to fight the problems of political corruption and other obstacles in becoming a mature nation.

West Pakistan has been much more carefully occupied by missions in the last few years than has East Pakistan, although the majority of the population of 84 million is in East Pakistan. There are no major areas left in West Pakistan that have not been entered by mission societies in the last few years. The work as a whole in West Pakistan is thoroughly conservative and has been surprisingly fruitful. The missions working in East Pakistan are less numerous with smaller missionary staff, and there has not been as much response. There are presently some 700 missionaries in Pakistan and approximately the same number of national workers. The Christian community is in the vicinity of 300,000.

Several areas of Pakistan are closed to missionary occupation because of military restrictions on the borders of Tibet and Russia, and in some of these areas there are tribes that have not been reached.

INDIA

This great nation of almost 400 million with its ancient culture and overwhelming religion has long challenged the

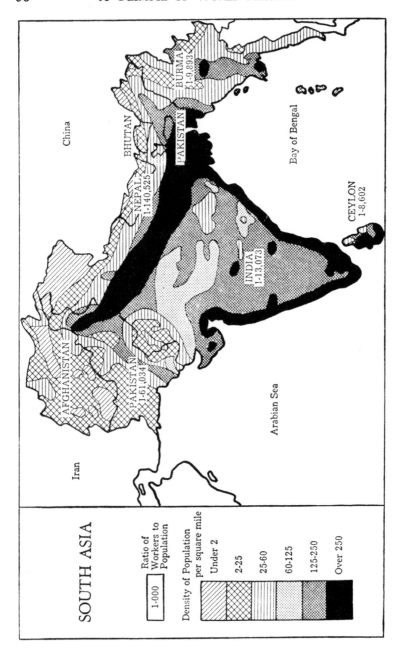

SOUTH ASIA

1-000   Ratio of
         Workers to
         Population

Density of Population
per square mile

Under 2

2-25

25-60

60-125

125-250

Over 250

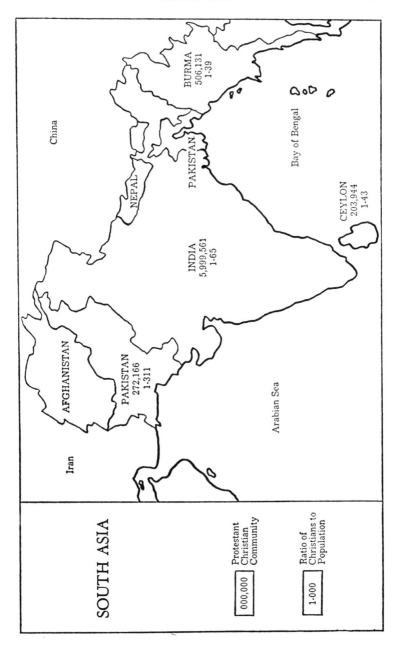

SOUTH ASIA

AFGHANISTAN

PAKISTAN
272,166
1-311

INDIA
5,999,561
1-65

PAKISTAN

NEPAL

China

BURMA
506,131
1-39

CEYLON
203,944
1-43

Bay of Bengal

Arabian Sea

Iran

| 000,000 | Protestant Christian Community |
| 1-000 | Ratio of Christians to Population |

friends of world evangelism. Of these millions only about 8 per cent live in cities and towns; the remaining 92 per cent live in hundreds of thousands of villages dotting the plains, plateaus and mountains. It is probable that at least 80 per cent of these villages have never been reached with the Gospel.

Linguistically, India is something of a problem. There does not seem to be any accurate statement on the actual number of Indian languages and dialects, but there are at least 27 languages and over 300 dialects. Some of these are well within the interior of India; many are in border areas. For example, in the Kashmir state, which is currently under controversy as to whether it should belong to West Pakistan or India, there are several tribes closed to missionary occupation, but in whose language small portions of the Scriptures have been translated. There is one tribe of approximately 2 million that has no Christian missionary working among them and no Scripture translation whatsoever.

Along the Tibetan border and in northeast India, Assam, and other areas, there are a number of tribes with no Scriptures in their language, although many of these have at least been contacted for the Gospel.

Under the present government of India, a determined effort is being made in the interest of nationalism to eliminate all foreigners whose occupation or work can be done by nationals. The India government recently quoted figures indicating that approximately 1,200 of the 5,500 missionaries who were in India in 1957 have been eliminated from India. This has largely been done by refusing new visas and in some cases refusing to grant re-entry permits. The missionary staff at the present time, therefore, is probably somewhat over 4,000.

There have been some revivals among certain Indian

Hindu sects that offer something of a problem to the work of Christianizing the people. In the southern province of Kerala, the Communists have seized control in an area where the Mar Thoma church has numerous members. There are approximately 6 million Protestant Christians in India, of whom not more than 2 million are active in the Protestant Church. However, it is readily admitted that given a revival in the church and a strong lay movement, the church in India could very well complete the evangelization of the nation.

One of the very bright spots in India is the establishment of a Union Theological Seminary that is receiving the cooperation of a large number of evangelical missions. It is the largest theological seminary in India, thoroughly evangelical, with very high educational standards, and is producing exceptional men as pastors and missionaries to work in India and the surrounding countries. When the last survey was taken there were over 90 foreign organizations working in India, in addition to a number of Indian national churches.

BURMA

Whereas India was the birthplace of Buddhism there are relatively few Buddhists left in India, it being a Hindu country. But it has exported Buddhism to the rest of South and Southeast Asia. It is said that the purest Buddhism is found in Burma. This was encountered by the earliest missionaries entering there and proved to be a formidable foe to the Gospel. Actually, Buddhism is almost as impregnable to the Gospel as is Islam.

Burma is roughly divided into two sections—the lower or costal areas (heavily Buddhist), and the northern and mountain sections (populated by at least 85 tribes—mostly animists, with the exception of the largest tribe, the Shans, who

are Buddhists). Eventually the Gospel reached the hill country, and it was here that a great majority of the converts to
Christianity were made. Of the more than 500,000 Christians
in Burma, a very great majority are among the hill people.

The missionary staff in Burma has been greatly reduced
since World War II, and it is difficult to get in new missionaries. New mission agencies are not allowed to enter. Some
institutions closed by World War II have not been allowed
to reopen. There are currently about 150 missionaries working in Burma with almost 2,000 national workers.

CEYLON

The beautiful island of Ceylon at the tip of India is another very interesting mission field with almost 9 million people and an area of 25,000 square miles. The population
density is very high. The country having been a colony of
both Holland and England, foreign missions have had free
access in years gone by, yet today the population of Ceylon is
only slightly over 1 per cent Christian, while Buddhism
claims 61 per cent of the people, Hinduism 22 per cent, Mo-
hammedanism 7 per cent, and other religions 9 per cent. The
largest concentration of Christians is in the vicinity of the
capital, Colombo, and the strongest Christian churches are
the Reformed and Anglican.

The present government is strongly Buddhist. Buddhism
in Ceylon is nontheistic. The Hindu minority is large
enough to have considerable strength and there are frequent
clashes between the Hindus and the Buddhists, particularly
in North Ceylon where the Hindus have come to work on
the plantations. When these religious clashes take place the
Christian minority, as well as others are greatly endangered.
The present government of Ceylon is not allowing the

entrance of new mission societies; and the entrance of new missionaries, except as replacements, has been greatly restricted.

NEPAL

This little kingdom nestled among the Himalayan mountains is one of the most recently opened for Christian activity. The religion is a combination of Buddhism and Hinduism, with the sex worship of Hinduism more strongly emphasized in Nepal than in India. Education and medical missions have been allowed entrance into Nepal. A joint venture of several societies has provided a number of clinics and hospitals in the country, as well as several schools. Roman Catholics have also entered, putting their entire emphasis on education.

In addition to those moving into the interior of the country, missions that have worked for years on the border have now been able to see their witness advance into the country itself. At the present time there are several small congregations, with possibly two or three hundred Nepalese Christians. The country is not open for missionary work which has proselytism as its purpose. As the door opens there will be some linguistic problems, although Nepali is the principal language of the country.

BHUTAN

The little kingdom of Bhutan, also nestling on the north border of India among the Himalayas, is closed to missionary endeavor. The only missionary activities related to this land are the missions on its border that are endeavoring to reach those from Bhutan who cross over into India. This is a sensitive area because of its proximity to Tibet and Communist China.

SOUTHEAST ASIA

SOUTHEAST ASIA is that section of territory east of Burma and south of China, extending as a peninsula down toward Indonesia. This area includes the countries of Thailand, Laos, Cambodia, Vietnam, and Malaya, with the Crown city of Singapore at the bottom. Until a few years ago this area, with a population of over 55 millions, was one of the most neglected areas in the world. However, since World War II, hundreds of missionaries have come into this area, including many who had to leave China. These are not only reaching the Chinese in Southeast Asia, but are in the process of reaching a number of the tribespeople. Whereas there were comparatively few missionaries in 1952, now there are over 1,000 missionaries in the area, and 850 national workers. Malaya is largely Muslim and all the other countries are predominantly Buddhist, except for the primitive tribespeople who are animists.

THAILAND

Known as Siam for many years, Thailand is called the "Rice Bowl" of Southeast Asia. It is mainly a Buddhist country. The northern part, however, is largely animistic, and there are four small Muslim provinces in the south.

In all of Thailand there are said to be about 20,000 baptized Christians and a Christian community of about 30,000. But in Thailand there are 20,000 Buddhist temples—one

SOUTHEAST ASIA

Country	Population	Church Members	Christian Community
Cambodia,	4,740,000		
Laos and	1,655,000		
Vietnam (S.)	12,300,000	14,964	45,000
Malaya	6,058,317	26,246	54,334
Thailand	21,076,000	20,736	28,775
Totals	45,829,317	61,946	128,109

SOUTHEAST ASIA—*Cont.*

	Native Staff	Foreign Staff	Ratio—Christians to Population	Ratio—Workers to Population
Cambodia,	..	..	..	..
Laos and	..	..	..	..
Vietnam (S.)	296	146	1- 415	1- 4,230
Malaya	298	395	1- 111	1- 8,742
Thailand	238	483	1- 732	1- 29,232
Totals	832	1,024	1- 357	1- 24,687

temple to each baptized Christian—and there are approximately 200,000 Buddhist monks. In spite of the tremendous influence of Buddhism and the fact that it is a state religion, there is religious freedom in the country, even to the extent that a number of the radio stations permit Gospel broadcasting.

Prior to World War II, only two major missions were active in Thailand. Since then, mission societies have entered all but four or five of the provinces, so that today every major area of Thailand is within the scope of one of the existing missions. From approximately 150 missionaries at the time of World War II, the missionary staff has increased to about 500. There are several theological training schools, a large number of primary schools, and some secondary schools. There are organized churches for leprosy patients in the country, and even a Bible institute for them.

In general, the picture of Thailand is a hopeful one and,

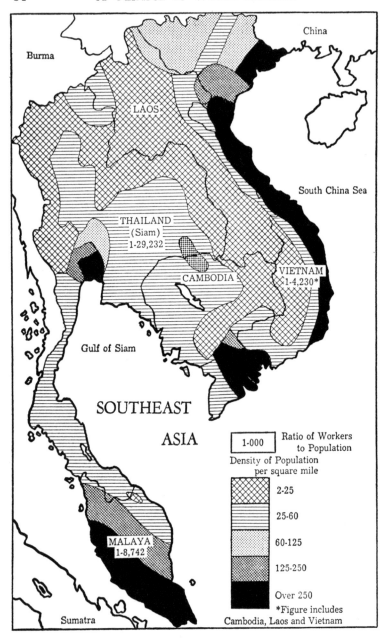

China

Burma

LAOS×

South China Sea

THAILAND
(Siam)
1-29,232

CAMBODIA

VIETNAM
‹1-4,230*

Gulf of Siam

SOUTHEAST

ASIA

| 1-000 | Ratio of Workers to Population |

Density of Population
per square mile

2-25

25-60

60-125

125-250

Over 250

*Figure includes
Cambodia, Laos and Vietnam

MALAYA
1-8,742

Sumatra

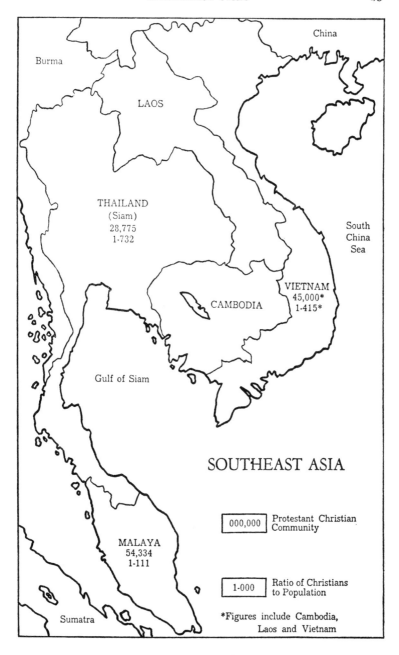

China

Burma

LAOS

THAILAND
(Siam)
28,775
1-732

South
China
Sea

VIETNAM
45,000*
1-415*

CAMBODIA

Gulf of Siam

SOUTHEAST ASIA

| 000,000 | Protestant Christian Community |

MALAYA
54,334
1-111

| 1-000 | Ratio of Christians to Population |

*Figures include Cambodia,
Laos and Vietnam

Sumatra

aside from the Buddhists' built-in resistance, we can expect an excellent harvest for the Gospel.

INDO-CHINA

This is the former name of an area that now comprises four countries—Laos, Cambodia, Vietnam, and Vietminh (North Vietnam). The latter is the section of Vietnam which was taken by the Communists. It is closed to the Gospel, but Vietnam, which has the majority of the people of the country, is wide open. Laos, Cambodia and Vietnam are all nominally Buddhist, but not always to the same degree. Vietnam is less Buddhist, partially due to a higher degree of modern civilization and commerce, partially due to the fact that the Presidential family and many of those in high office are Roman Catholics, but largely due to the fact that Vietnam was highly infiltrated by the French during the time it was a colony. All three have a number of tribes, with missionaries working among many of them. Several new missions have entered Laos, and there are prospects of other missions entering Cambodia and Vietnam.

In this area there are approximately 120 tribes and dialects that must be reached with the Gospel. Of these, perhaps 25 languages and dialects have some translation of the Scriptures. The rest still remain to be reached in their native tongue.

The major mission in Vietnam has one whole segment of the church and several schools directed exclusively toward the tribes, and all the members of the church in that area are converts from the various tribes. Other training schools for the Vietnamese are operated on the coast.

In general, the response to the Gospel has been good. The least responsive are the people of Cambodia, perhaps because this is the most fanatically Buddhist of the three countries.

The country of South Vietnam has been dedicated to the Virgin Mary by the Catholic minority in the country. This, however, has not hindered the ministry of the Protestant missions, with the exception of some totally Catholic villages where the missionaries and evangelists are not welcome.

In recent years, there has been a great drive for literacy in this whole area and the door is opening more and more to the Gospel. Of course, the constant threat is the march of Communism from the north.

MALAYA

The southern tip of this peninsula is occupied by one of the newer countries of the world, the sovereign monarchy that has remained within the British Commonwealth. The principal inhabitants are the Malays, who are almost all Muslims. The Muslim faith is the religion of the nation. However, there are sizable minorities of Chinese and Tamil-speaking people from India. The Chinese are being used by the Communists as the agents through whom they would infiltrate the country.

Now, the Malayan government has opened the country for missionary work among all but Malays. They may not be proselytized because they are Muslims. In an attempt to stop Communist activity, the new government has assembled the Chinese of Malaya into a large number of modern villages. There are about 600 of these villages, numbering anywhere from 200 to 10,000 people in each one. There are resident Gospel workers now in about 100 of these villages, with another 100 being reached from outside. Work among these Chinese has been carried on for many years and the Christian community in Malaya, including Singapore, is about 97 per cent Chinese. There have been a number of schools operated so that today the Christian constituency in all of Malaya is about 50,000, 30,000 of them living in the Crown Colony of Singapore.

The island of Singapore, a Crown Colony but still considered a part of Malaya, is very interesting from the missionary viewpoint. In addition to a number of small agencies, there are 14 English-speaking churches and 34 Chinese-speaking churches on the island. The Chinese churches are organized into an interchurch union, which is strongly evangelical. It is operating the Singapore Theological Seminary which promises to be of tremendous influence in this whole section of the world. Of course, the big threat to the over-all program in Singapore is that of Communism, because the Communist Party is very powerful in this section of the world.

Singapore has perhaps one of the highest birth rates in the world—60 per cent of the population is under twenty-one years of age. It is said that there are 1,275 babies born per week in Singapore. The government would have to open one new school for 1,000 children every week if they were to keep up with the present increase in population. An excellent work is being done among the high school students of this area through Bible retreats, special Bible classes and youth evangelism with the Chinese young people going out as Gospel teams all over the city. It has highlighted the fact that probably one of the great weaknesses in work elsewhere is the failure to reach the youth and children, who comprise the bulk of the population.

It is not easy for new mission agencies to enter the work either in Singapore or in the peninsula proper in Malaya. It is necessary for the mission to be sponsored by someone already in the area. However, agencies or missionaries already recognized by the government apparently enter without difficulty.

EAST ASIA OR THE FAR EAST

FOR MANY YEARS, in considering East Asia, or the Far East, we always thought of the great country of China and Manchuria and all of Korea. So, even though we are not including China and North Korea in our tables, we shall comment on them here. Also, since the Philippines are generally associated with the Far East in our thinking, they will be included here but will be shown on the map of the Island World.

FAR EAST

Country	Population	Church Members	Christian Community
Formosa	7,647,703	73,393	155,294
Hong Kong	2,340,000	55,237	100,000
Japan	88,900,000	266,652	350,000
Philippines	21,000,000	1,791,556	3,721,019
South Korea	25,120,174	293,806	844,377
Totals	145,007,877	2,480,644	5,170,690

FAR EAST—Cont.

	Native Staff	Foreign Staff	Ratio—Christians to Population	Ratio—Workers to Population
Formosa	375	353	1- 49	1- 10,505
Hong Kong	250	245	1- 23	1- 4,727
Japan	3,783	3,731	1- 254	1- 11,831
Philippines	2,992	774	1- 5	1- 5,576
South Korea	3,357	418	1- 30	1- 6,654
Totals	10,757	5,521	1- 28	1- 8,957

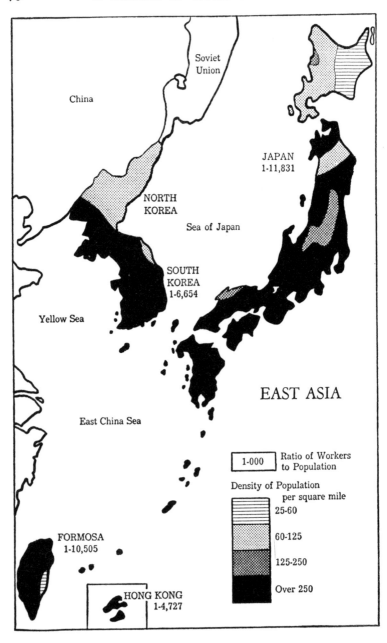

Soviet
Union

China

JAPAN
1-11,831

NORTH
KOREA

Sea of Japan

SOUTH
KOREA
1-6,654

Yellow Sea

EAST ASIA

East China Sea

| 1-000 | Ratio of Workers to Population |

Density of Population
per square mile

25-60

60-125

125-250

Over 250

FORMOSA
1-10,505

HONG KONG
1-4,727

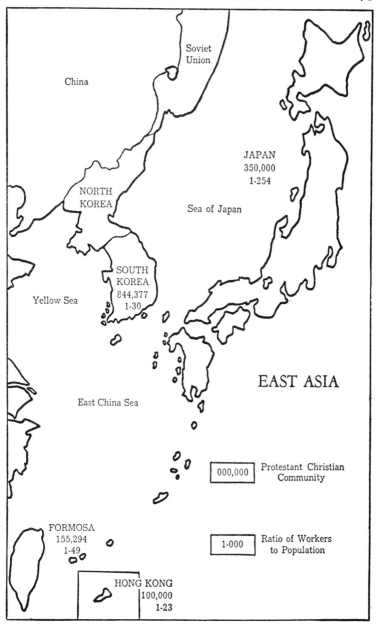

Soviet
Union

China

JAPAN
350,000
1-254

NORTH
KOREA

Sea of Japan

SOUTH
KOREA
844,377
1-30

Yellow Sea

EAST ASIA

East China Sea

000,000   Protestant Christian
Community

FORMOSA
155,294
1-49

1-000   Ratio of Workers
to Population

HONG KONG
100,000
1-23

COMMUNIST CHINA

Information about the Christian Church in Communist China is incomplete. We are told that this great land, including Manchuria and Mongolia, now has more than 600 million inhabitants.

It is estimated that there were approximately 1 million baptized church members in China at the time of the Communist occupation. There were nearly 12,000 churches, thousands of other places of worship, and over 10,000 national workers. More than 2 million people called themselves Protestant Christians, in addition to several million Roman Catholics in the country. Since that time, of course, China has taken in Outer China, including Tibet, and has extended its influence down into North Vietnam. These people originally practiced the religions of Confucianism, Taoism and Buddhism. In West China there were several million Chinese Muslims, and many tribal religions in the southwest. All of these religions have been taken over to a degree by the Communist regime. Most of these areas had had the Gospel witness, with the exception of a number of tribes in the southwest that did not receive the Gospel in their own language.

Today the church in China continues to exist. It has lost a great number of its pastors, especially those who were true to the faith. The church has been taken over officially by the government in the Three Self Movement. In large cities, such as Peking and Shanghai, not more than 5 per cent of the churches remain open. Those that do function continue to have amazing results, particularly those where the Gospel is still preached. All Christian institutions have been taken over by the government. No one knows the actual number of those who have remained true to the faith.

The greatest ministry the Church of Jesus Christ can have

today in China is to pray for God's children there, that they may be kept faithful and may have a real witness for the Gospel in the midst of much opposition.

NORTH KOREA

The reports from North Korea are far more tragic than those from China. Information received states that there are no churches functioning in North Korea where the population is about 9 million. This area that once had perhaps 70 per cent of the total Christian community in Korea is now without any open witness whatever. What Christianity exists must be underground. As far as we can understand, all known preachers of the Gospel in North Korea have been either liquidated or deported.

FORMOSA

Now we come to the open areas of the Far East and we start first with Formosa.

This beautiful island of over 9 million Formosans and mainland Chinese, including quite a few thousand native tribespeople, is currently operated as Nationalist China. It is wide open to the Gospel, and since World War II around 400 missionaries have entered. At the time of the last census 1 per cent of the population were church members; more than 2 per cent were professing Christians. There were just about as many national workers as missionaries. A number of Bible schools and several seminaries have been opened, and two Christian colleges have been started. At least a score of clinics and hospitals are being operated, many of them in a specialized way for the tribespeople of Formosa who have a high incidence of tuberculosis. Evangelistic campaigns have been held in many sections of the island and a strong Sunday School movement has started. In this area the Christian population has increased approximately 100 per cent in five years. It is said that the greatest need in Formosa now is time to accomplish the task. There is an excellent staff to do the work.

HONG KONG

The Crown Colony of Hong Kong comprises the island of Hong Kong, Stonecutters' Island, the Kowloon Peninsula, and the New Territories on the adjoining mainland. There are over $2\frac{1}{2}$ million people in this over-all city, with thousands of refugees arriving constantly from the mainland. Here are some of the most crowded communities in the world. For example, in one of the new refugee sections in Kowloon, 67.000 Chinese are living in an area of eight square blocks. They are housed in seven-story apartment buildings, with each apartment consisting of one 10 x 12 room. A large number of missions have entered here, with a total personnel in excess of 250 and at least that many national workers. A number of Bible institutes and seminaries are operated for the training of Chinese workers, not only for the colony itself, but to reach overseas Chinese. Due to the huge influx of refugees with thousands of children, the government has encouraged mission agencies to operate primary and secondary schools. The Roman Catholics have put a heavy emphasis on this program subsidized by the government, and so have some Protestant agencies. With all of this, only a portion of the children are cared for educationally.

The roof tops of the seven-story refugee apartment buildings are loaned for educational work. Various missions take certain buildings, adding rooms on top of the buildings for classes and leaving some of the area open for playgrounds. Much relief work is done by the various mission agencies operating through several over-all relief facilities. Where open-air evangelism is tried, and even in churches themselves, the response is most gratifying. There is great enthusiasm on the part of all who are evangelizing here, although the task seems hopelessly large.

Since this colony could be overrun by the Communists at their will, there is often speculation as to the worthwhileness of putting up churches, schools and other buildings, but the program pushes ahead. There are several orphanages operated in Hong Kong, and several large presses are producing material in Chinese and other languages for distribution all over Asia. One of the problems is, of course, the great variety of Chinese languages that are spoken, and this in itself makes necessary the reaching of people by language groups.

SOUTH KOREA

Free Korea has a population of about 22 million people. There are approximately 850,000 Protestant Christians and 5,300 churches. It is interesting to note that out of a population of 22 million there are less than 1 million Christians, 3½ million Buddhists, 1½ million Confucianists, making a total of 6 million people. Apparently, the rest of the people practice no religion.

The growth of the Christian Church in South Korea since the Korean war has been absolutely fantastic. New churches are being formed all the time. Although the church has now settled down to a more or less normal state, and there is no longer the tense excitement and drive that existed in the postwar days, there is still a tremendous program of evangelism going on. The national church in Korea is overwhelmingly evangelical and has some of the best-trained leaders in the Orient. There are several excellent seminaries operating in Korea, and a number of Bible institutes. Korea has been a prime example to the world in the indigenous church development. Several new missions have entered in recent years, but the predominant drive and force of the work is still with the older denominations that were working there prior to World War II.

JAPAN

Japan, a land about the size of the State of Montana, has 91 million people with about 8½ million living in the city of Tokyo. With the freedom following World War II a great number of missionaries entered, so that according to the last survey there were approximately 3,700 foreign missionaries in Japan. Of these the overwhelming majority are thoroughgoing evangelicals with a conservative Protestant message. The total Protestant population of Japan is probably in the vicinity of 350,000. But while this modest growth has been taking place Buddhism has grown until there are 170 Buddhist sects in Japan, with almost 130,000 priests presiding over 90,000 temples where approximately 43 million worship. At the same time Shintoism has been developing, and between the two forms of Shinto they now have 142 sects with 192,000 priests in charge of 116,000 shrines and churches ministering to about 89 million Japanese. Of course, there is an overlap here, as many of the Japanese are adherents of both Buddhism and Shintoism.

In addition, a survey made by the Japanese Ministry of Education indicates that there are at least 120 new religions, with 17,000 teachers officiating in 12,000 meeting places, and about 11 million adherents.

In the midst of all of this Protestants have gone ahead, especially evangelicals, with a strong program of evangelism. Bible institutes and several Christian colleges have been established with the purpose of building a strong evangelical church in Japan. Although the growth of the church has been disappointing to many, we believe a new day is dawning in the use of both team evangelism and mass evangelistic meetings, plus all of the other media being used to get the Gospel out to this great dynamic country. There does seem to be need of a better distribution of missionaries, more effective comity, and a real effort to develop a Christian society that will overcome the old Japanese feudalistic system, which until now has largely dominated the church and its social institutions.

OKINAWA

As we move toward the Philippines, we should make mention of Okinawa and its sister islands. These islands, Japanese-controlled prior to World War II and now a United Nations' trusteeship under the control of the United States, have a population of approximately 500,000. Previously, they were to a large degree the object of one missionary society's endeavor. Now there are three or four mission agencies working there. A number of the inhabitants have been led to Jesus Christ and new churches are being developed.

THE PHILIPPINES

In the Philippines, 7,000 islands and an estimated 55 major languages and 148 dialects and sub-dialects challenge the 42 missionary and church agencies with a missionary staff of almost 800 and 3,000 national workers who are endeavoring to accomplish the tremendous task. Transportation between the many islands is one problem. The exceedingly mountainous terrain, with small tribes hidden away in the mountains, is another. A real drive is taking place at the present time to care for some of the greatest linguistic needs of the island. In a population of 20 million there are almost 4 million Protestants, and church membership is approaching the 2 million mark. Many of these churches are now well organized, completely self-supporting, and some have started to send missionaries to other lands. There is still much pioneer work to be done, but we believe the Philippine Church should be challenged with the task of reaching its own people. There is, without doubt, room for a number of linguists and others to help finish the task on the Philippine Islands. Apart from the small areas occupied by these illiterate tribes, there is none that would be large enough to demand the work of another mission.

INDONESIA AND THE ISLAND WORLD

GEOGRAPHICALLY, Indonesia includes not only the Republic of Indonesia with all its member islands stretching for a distance of almost 3,000 miles from east of Singapore to New Guinea, but it also includes the island of New Guinea, the sections of North Borneo that are not in the Indonesian Republic, and other minor islands in the area. In addition to these are three groups of islands: Micronesia (the islands north of the equator and west of the international dateline), Melanesia (the islands south of the equator and west of the international dateline), and Polynesia (all the islands east of the international dateline). These are spread over an area of more than 4,000 miles from north to south, and more than 8,000 miles from east to west. However, most of the islands are very small and the population of the three main groups totals approximately 3 million. The Republic of Indonesia has a population of approximately 85 million, and there are something over a million in the rest of this Indonesian area including New Guinea.

Missionary work throughout this entire area is quite a romantic tale. For the most part the original encounters were with head-hunters and with every manifestation of degenerate religions. The Muslims moved in and, with the exception of Bali which is predominantly Hindu, Indonesia is very largely Mohammedan. The islands of Polynesia, Melanesia and Micronesia, except where Roman Catholicism was introduced by Catholic colonial governments, or in a few cases where the Muslim faith spread over from Indonesia, all had animistic or pagan religions, many of them embodying aspects of ancestor worship, frequently with a very complicated set of taboos. The islands had varying degrees of morality and head-hunting was a common practice. Cannibalism was encountered in many of the islands and still prevails in a few places.

First, we will consider the Republic of Indonesia; second, New Guinea as an entity (although it is divided into three sections) and North Borneo; third, the small islands of the Pacific.

INDONESIA AND THE ISLAND WORLD

Country	Population	Church Members	Christian Community
Indonesia	85,500,000	520,000	3,125,000
New Guinea	775,000	31,431	103,000
North Borneo	395,000	19,871	51,187
Polynesia	751,210	71,698	262,290
Melanesia	1,894,184	181,761	461,399
Micronesia	496,670	58,386	183,589
Totals	89,812,064	883,147	4,186,465

INDONESIA AND THE ISLAND WORLD—Cont.

	Native Staff	Foreign Staff	Ratio—Christians to Population	Ratio—Workers to Population
Indonesia	4,150	250	1- 27	1- 19,431
New Guinea	385	225	1- 7	1- 1,270
North Borneo	77	9	1- 7	1- 4,593
Polynesia	1,248	241	1- 2	1- 504
Melanesia	5,464	726	1- 4	1- 306
Micronesia	716	100	1- 2	1- 608
Totals	12,040	1,551	1- 21	1- 6,608

INDONESIA

After Indonesia came under colonial control Protestantism made a great advance throughout the entire area, with the result that more Muslims have been won to Christ on these islands than in any other section of the world, and today they are more accessible to the Gospel than any others. However, in Indonesia there are still some pagan areas that have not been reached, particularly in the interior of Borneo and Celebes, and there are some larger sections of Sumatra and a few areas of Java that are not being reached with the Gospel. It should be noted that Indonesia is not one race of people but a multiplicity of races with numerous languages. Therefore, Indonesia is not inhabited by a homogeneous people, but by various tribes and groups that are not always friendly toward each other. Due to the exit of Dutch missionaries at the time of the independence of Indonesia there is quite a shortage of foreign staff. The national staff, however, is in general well educated and carrying on the work.

Since World War II a number of new missions have entered these islands. The difficulty now comes from the demand of the Indonesian government that missionaries coming in be sponsored by existing missionary agencies, and the granting of visas is relatively slow. This means that new missionary agencies will find it very difficult to enter any of these areas. The greatest need seems to be to enlarge the missionary staff and multiply as rapidly as possible the number of national workers in the existing evangelical agencies. There are probably more than 3 million professed Christians in these islands, with over a half million church members.

In a discussion of Indonesia, attention must be given to the Chinese minority. Due to the pressures of Indonesian and Chinese Communists the nationalist Chinese in Indonesia are undergoing considerable hardship. This is compli-

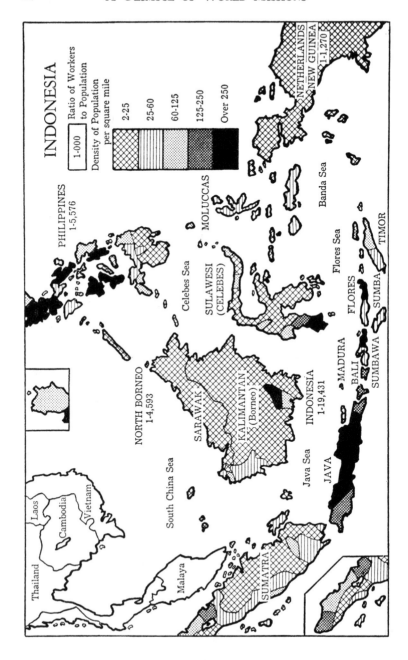

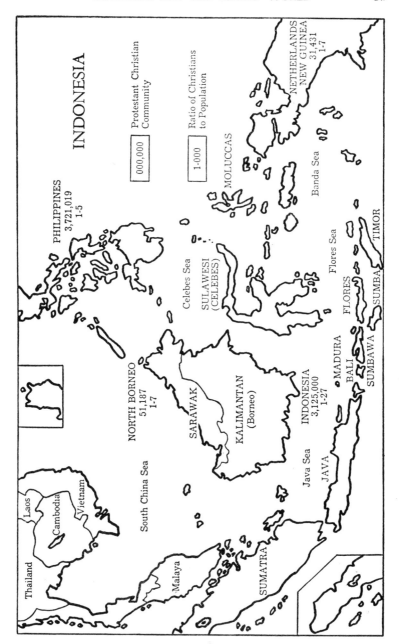

INDONESIA

Protestant Christian
Community

000,000

Ratio of Christians
to Population

1·000

NETHERLANDS
NEW GUINEA
31,431
1·7

MOLUCCAS

Banda Sea

PHILIPPINES
3,721,019
1·5

Celebes Sea

SULAWESI
(CELEBES)

Flores Sea

TIMOR

SUMBA

FLORES

NORTH BORNEO
51,187
1·7

SARAWAK

KALIMANTAN
(Borneo)

INDONESIA
3,125,000
1·27

MADURA

BALI

SUMBAWA

South China Sea

Java Sea

JAVA

Laos

Cambodia

Vietnam

Thailand

Malaya

SUMATRA

cated, furthermore, by the fact that under the Dutch regime the Chinese secured virtual control of commerce in many of the outlying sections of Indonesia, and even in the main cities they were the commercial leaders and had much of the finance of the islands in their control. In an effort to wrest their possessions from them the picture has become quite confused today. Some of the Chinese Christian schools are closed and many of the Chinese Christian leaders have had to leave the country. However, there has been an excellent response to the Gospel among the several million Chinese in Indonesia. In some areas they have operated their own training schools to provide pastors for their own churches and education for their own children.

There are still some languages in Indonesia that have not been reduced to writing and in which the people have no portion of God's Word. At the moment no effort is being made to reach many of these tribes.

Due to political and military violence in some sections of Indonesia, travel restrictions have been imposed which have made communications very difficult between the islands. For the most part surface travel has been stopped and air travel is limited. Economic controls, such as insisting that all materials printed in the Indonesian languages be printed in Indonesia, also have further complicated the situation. In the past the great bulk of Christian literature in this section of the world has been printed in either Singapore or Hong Kong. Thus the natural results of nationalism are apt to complicate the work of spreading the Gospel.

NEW GUINEA

Since World War II this beautiful mountainous island, currently under the jurisdiction of the Netherlands and Australia, has been the object of much missionary endeavor.

There are today almost as many missionaries in New Guinea as there are in all of the Indonesian Republic. The national staff in New Guinea, however, is quite limited.

With a total population of approximately 2 million people, over 1,200 languages have been discovered on this island. Missions are working on the task of reducing a number of these languages to writing, and efforts are being made to give them translations of the Scriptures. However, at the present rate it will be many years before all these individual tribes have been reached with the message of the Gospel.

According to the last survey, there was a Christian community of something over 100,000. However, in the last few years there has been a notable response among these tribespeople and a number of new tribes have been reached.

The interior of New Guinea, still one of the great pioneer areas of the world, is going to need a number of linguists if these people are all to be reached with the Gospel.

BRITISH BORNEO

This area should be mentioned in passing. There are four or five mission agencies working in the northern third of Borneo, with quite a response to the Gospel, so that approximately 15 per cent of the population has professed faith in Jesus Christ. There is an estimated population of 400,000 people and about 160 Christian workers. There is still some linguistic work to be done.

THE PACIFIC ISLANDS

These three groups of islands, extending from those in the vicinity of Indonesia to the Hawaiian Islands, have received more missionary attention per capita than almost any other section of the world. The result is that there are very few islands of any size that do not have a Christian witness today.

Considering the entire group as a whole, approximately 30 per cent of the population are professed Christians.

There are more than 100 language groups scattered throughout these islands, many of whom do not have any translation of the Scriptures as yet. A large percentage, however, do have at least a part of the Bible in their language and many of them have been reached by using related languages and dialects, or pidgin English.

The great bulk of Protestants are found on the islands that have been under British, Australian, New Zealand, Netherlands or United States influence. Those islands that have been largely under the control of Catholic colonial governments have not had as much opportunity to hear the Gospel.

LATIN AMERICA

THIS AREA WILL INCLUDE all republics and colonies south of the United States, starting with the Mexican border and including all Caribbean and South American countries. We will consider these in three areas—Mexico and Central America, the Caribbean, and South America. However, since a great majority of these Latin American countries are so similar in government, culture, and religion it will save time to look at their similarities before considering them separately. Spanish is the language of the great majority of these countries, the exception being Brazil where the language is Portuguese, and the colonies in the Caribbean area which have French or English-speaking groups.

All of the Spanish-speaking countries and Brazil are the product of Roman Catholic culture, and a majority of the people in each of these countries are Roman Catholics.

Politically, these countries are republics patterned after the United States and thus freedom of religion is guaranteed. This, however, is interpreted as anything from a mild tolerance to absolute freedom. In Mexico a reaction against clerical and church domination of the country has led to such extreme separation of church and state that there is really not complete freedom for foreign clergy in Mexico. Foreign clergy are allowed in Mexico, but they are not allowed to perform the sacerdotal functions. These must be done by native clergy. This is true of Catholics, Protestants, and

LATIN AMERICA

Country	Population	Church Members	Christian Community
Argentina	19,858,000	116,557	364,369
Bahamas	116,530	19,507	41,580
Bolivia	3,273,000	11,240	29,373
Brazil	61,268,000	809,576	2,175,927
British Guiana	508,000	45,103	151,504
British Honduras	82,000	6,174	27,186
Chile	7,121,000	133,180	370,428
Colombia	13,227,000	14,317	60,400
Costa Rica	1,035,000	4,847	10,992
Cuba	6,410,000	47,995	215,732
Dominican Republic	2,698,000	10,091	25,802
Ecuador	3,890,000	2,669	4,888
El Salvador	2,268,464	10,406	29,198
Falkland Islands	2,230	1,500	2,000
French Guiana	27,863	70	162
Guatemala	3,450,000	28,956	142,465
Haiti	3,384,000	91,330	313,279
Honduras	1,711,000	6,724	24,758
Jamaica	1,579,620	143,584	653,742
Mexico	31,426,000	221,873	910,951
Nicaragua	1,331,000	12,598	37,666
Panama Republic and Canal Zone	1,012,822	23,630	47,722
Paraguay	1,638,000	3,441	22,839
Peru	9,923,000	28,922	72,789
Puerto Rico	2,281,000	48,136	147,411
Surinam	250,000	5,844	60,213
Trinidad and Tobago	743,000	44,864	222,457
Uruguay	2,650,000	8,047	16,663
Venezuela	6,134,000	8,690	17,766
Totals	189,298,529	2,155,323	6,189,031

others. Also, church property is held by the government for the church. This, of course, was a reaction against the immense property holdings of the Roman Catholic Church in comparison to the relative poverty of the people themselves.

These Latin American republics have inherited the problem that as colonies they were operated as totalitarian regimes, with absolute authority in the governor and a feuda-

LATIN AMERICA—*Cont.*

	Native Staff	Foreign Staff	Ratio—Christians to Population	Ratio—Workers to Population
Argentina	844	700	1- 55	1- 13,239
Bahamas	32	182	1- 2	1- 544
Bolivia	208	522	1- 111	1- 4,484
Brazil	5,950	979	1- 28	1- 8,841
British Guiana	556	426	1- 3	1- 517
British Honduras	38	33	1- 3	1- 1,155
Chile	351	289	1- 19	1- 11,127
Colombia	266	279	1- 219	1- 24,270
Costa Rica	109	122	1- 94	1- 4,481
Cuba	840	254	1- 30	1- 5,859
Dominican Republic	276	138	1- 104	1- 6,517
Ecuador	132	290	1- 796	1- 9,218
El Salvador	145	55	1- 78	1- 11,342
Falkland Islands	6	15	1- 1	1- 106
French Guiana	1	6	1- 172	1- 3,980
Guatemala	356	194	1- 24	1- 6,273
Haiti	880	523	1- 11	1- 2,412
Honduras	202	133	1- 69	1- 5,107
Jamaica	777	407	1- 2	1- 1,334
Mexico	1,385	551	1- 35	1- 16,232
Nicaragua	138	65	1- 35	1- 6,557
Panama Republic and Canal Zone	137	278	1- 21	1- 2,440
Paraguay	57	113	1- 72	1- 9,635
Peru	261	447	1- 136	1- 14,016
Puerto Rico	420	120	1- 15	1- 4,224
Surinam	75	42	1- 4	1- 2,137
Trinidad and Tobago	188	274	1- 3	1- 1,608
Uruguay	58	79	1- 160	1- 19,343
Venezuela	192	317	1- 345	1- 12,051
Totals	14,770	7,790	1- 30	1- 8,390

listic system in the field of economy. This program did not produce the type of citizen who can easily become self-governing. Frequently, the instability in these governments has resulted in dictatorships. At the moment, absolute dictatorships in Latin America are at a low ebb.

Whereas at one time these Latin American republics all had very close relationships with the Vatican, only three now

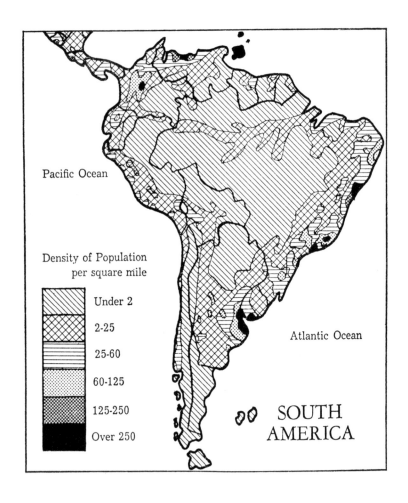

Pacific Ocean

Density of Population
per square mile

Under 2

2-25

25-60

60-125

125-250

Over 250

Atlantic Ocean

SOUTH
AMERICA

VENEZUELA
17,766
BRITISH GUIANA 151,504
SURINAM 60,213
FRENCH GUIANA
162
COLOMBIA
60,400
ECUADOR
4,888
BRAZIL
2,175,927
PERU
72,789
BOLIVIA
29,373
Pacific Ocean
PARAGUAY
22,839
CHILE
370,428
ARGENTINA
364,369
Atlantic Ocean
Figures Indicate
Protestant Christian
Community
URUGUAY
10,459
SOUTH
AMERICA
FALKLAND ISLANDS
2,230

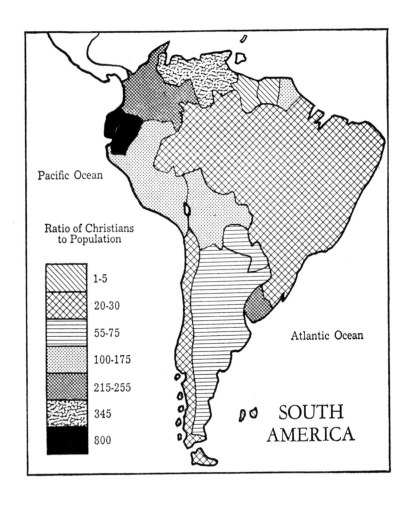

Pacific Ocean

Ratio of Christians
to Population

	1-5
	20-30
	55-75
	100-175
	215-255
	345
	800

Atlantic Ocean

SOUTH
AMERICA

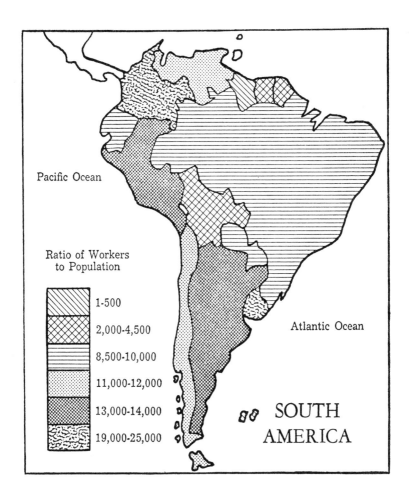

Pacific Ocean

Ratio of Workers
to Population

1-500

2,000-4,500

8,500-10,000

11,000-12,000

13,000-14,000

19,000-25,000

Atlantic Ocean

SOUTH
AMERICA

have an actual concordat (treaty) still in effect with the Vatican. Haiti has a concordat that was signed in 1860. Colombia has one signed in 1887, and the Dominican Republic has one signed in 1954. All others have either lapsed or were cancelled. Two countries have special agreements with the Vatican. Ecuador signed an agreement in 1937, and Bolivia signed one in 1957. In most of the other countries the Roman Catholic Church exerts considerable influence, because of the fact it has been a state religion and is a majority religion at the present time. In every case it is as active in politics as it is permitted to be and exerts as much influence as possible upon the public school systems.

It is noted that as long as the Roman Catholic Church has control of the educational system, illiteracy remains at a high level. Throughout Latin America great stress is being placed on education, with those countries most free from Roman Catholic control showing the greatest advances in literacy.

Politically, many of the countries are more stable now than they have been for a number of years. There is still a certain amount of instability in Colombia, due to the number of years of internal strife. The present coalition government is not as secure as it might be, but it is making every effort to return to a normal state of freedom and personal rights. Bolivia, facing an economic problem in nationalizing its main industries, has been severely threatened by Communist control, the worst enemy being terrific inflation. After years of dictatorship, Argentina is once more free and is seeking to overcome its economic problems. Religious freedom is ample, with the exception that missions are now required to register all of their meeting places and activities with the government.

Religious opposition is spotty throughout this entire area. In most of the countries, the incidents of persecution can be laid at the door of a local priest who is stirring up trouble. In Colombia, however, there has until recently been organized resistance, with attacks on the Protestant minority under the cover of the civil strife within the country. Approximately 117 Protestant pastors, church officials and teachers have been murdered. More than 200 schools have been closed and over 50 churches destroyed.

Approximately 65 per cent of the geographical territory of Colombia has been brought under the control of the Roman Catholic hierarchy by an agreement with the government, giving them exclusive rights to education and religious activities in this area. This has closed a number of Protestant churches, a very large number of schools, and caused considerable hardship on the Protestant minority in this area. At the time of this writing, the entire agreement is actually illegal because it has never been ratified by the Colombian Congress.

Roman Catholic influence in Latin America is definitely on the wane. Catholic reports indicate that the percentage of practicing Catholics ranges anywhere from 6 to 12 per cent.

Missionary Occupation

The last survey of Latin America indicates that the ratio of Protestant workers to population varies from 1 to 1,400 in Jamaica to 1 to 24,000 in Colombia, the latter being the least occupied of all the countries. This is explained in part, however, by the fact that for at least eight years no new missionaries were allowed to enter Colombia, and an effort was made to reduce the number already there as much as possible. At present new missionaries are succeeding in getting visas to enter Colombia.

There are eight countries in Latin America where there

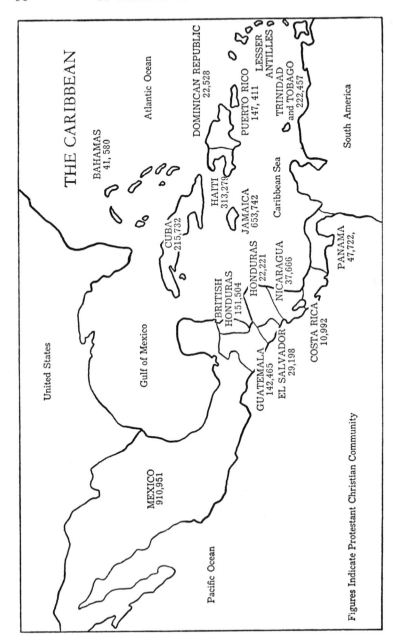

THE CARIBBEAN

BAHAMAS
41, 580

Atlantic Ocean

DOMINICAN REPUBLIC
22,528

PUERTO RICO
147, 411

LESSER
ANTILLES

TRINIDAD
and TOBAGO
222,457

South America

CUBA
215,732

HAITI
313,279

JAMAICA
653,742

Caribbean Sea

PANAMA
47,722,

BRITISH
HONDURAS
151,504

HONDURAS
22,221

NICARAGUA
37,666

COSTA RICA
10,992

GUATEMALA
142,465

EL SALVADOR
29,198

United States

Gulf of Mexico

MEXICO
910,951

Pacific Ocean

Figures Indicate Protestant Christian Community

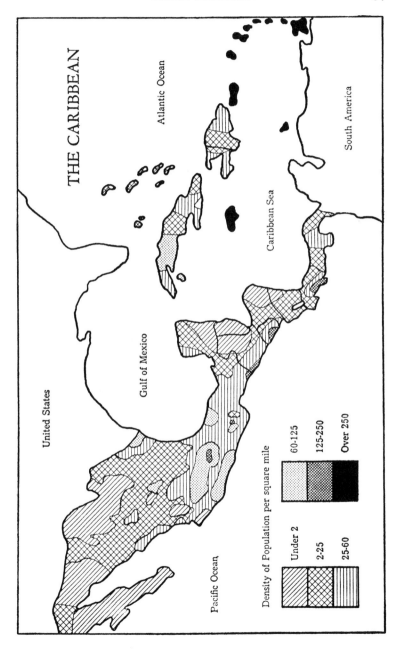

THE CARIBBEAN

United States

Atlantic Ocean

South America

Gulf of Mexico

Caribbean Sea

Pacific Ocean

Density of Population per square mile

Under 2
2-25
25-60
60-125
125-250
Over 250

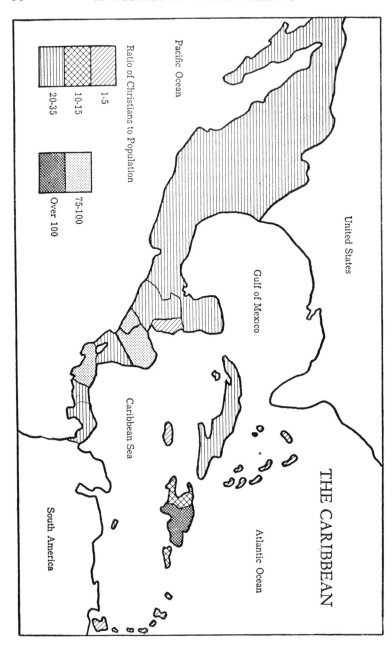

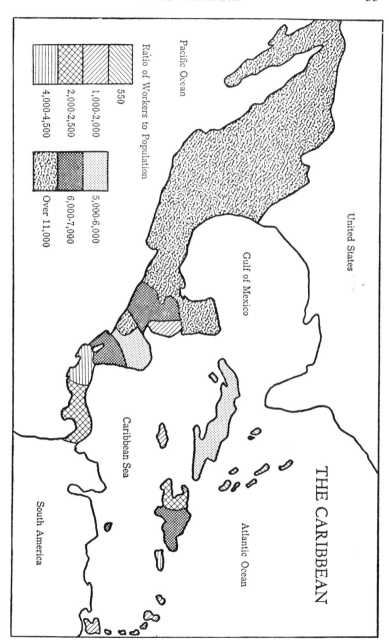

Pacific Ocean

Ratio of Workers to Population

550
1,000-2,000
2,000-2,500
4,000-4,500

5,000-6,000
6,000-7,000
Over 11,000

United States

Gulf of Mexico

Caribbean Sea

South America

Atlantic Ocean

THE CARIBBEAN

are 10,000 or more people per worker. Ecuador has one worker to 10,000; Peru has one to 11,000; Venezuela and El Salvador have one to 12,000; Argentina has one to almost 13,000; Mexico has one to 16,000; Uruguay has one to over 19,000; and Colombia has one to 24,000. This is not necessarily an index to the extent of missionary occupancy, however, since there is sometimes a concentration of missionaries in key centers.

Education

A large number of Bible institutes and some bona fide seminaries are operated by evangelical missions in the lands to the south. A few missions which have not previously done so are now undertaking to establish secondary schools. At present there is no thoroughgoing evangelical arts college in all of Latin America. However, an increasing number of evangelical students are taking courses in the state universities. In the areas where we have older and better developed churches, such as Brazil, Argentina, Chile and Mexico, the educational standards of the clergy show marked superiority over those of other areas.

Linguistics

During the last twenty-five years, a tremendous drive has been made from Mexico on southward across all of Latin America to reduce the tribal languages to writing and give them some of God's Word. Although there is no completely accurate survey of the linguistic problem, there are probably over 275 tribal languages in Latin America (mostly in South America) that have no Scripture translation, and for the most part these languages have not been reduced to writing. However, it is known that many of these languages belong to small tribes with less than 500 members. Quite a few have less than 100 members. It is also known that many of these are being reached through Portuguese or Spanish, as the tribes having contact with civilization quickly pick up the other language. However, after eliminating all these there are still a hundred or more languages that need to be reduced to writing and have the Scriptures translated.

Opportunities for Work in Latin America

WEST INDIES

For the most part, the islands of the West Indies are well supplied with missionaries and national workers. Some of the French islands have only recently allowed the entrance of missionaries with complete freedom. In others, such as Haiti, so many mission agencies have entered that efforts to find an area in which to work causes a comity problem. The British islands seem to be well supplied with workers, so the demand is not great.

MEXICO AND CENTRAL AMERICA

In Mexico and Central America it is a different story. In Mexico we face the problem that missionaries as such are not granted visas. The only way they can enter is as tourists, and then they must come out every six months for renewal of their visas. There are only a little over 1,900 workers in all of Mexico to reach 31 million people.

The other republics in Central America are open to missionary work and all of them are better staffed than Mexico. There are seemingly adequate numbers of missionary societies working in these countries.

SOUTH AMERICA

The slowest work in Latin America is among the Indians, particularly the Quechuas who are quite numerous down through Ecuador, Peru and Bolivia. They seem to have been rather slow to accept the Gospel. The work among the Latin Americans themselves has been much more fruitful.

A rather careful check of all of Latin America fails to find any sizable area untouched by the Gospel, but there are many smaller areas that need to be reached. Reports on Latin America indicate that this is one of the most fruitful mission fields of the world, with the Christian population increasing by 60 per cent in five years. With Roman Catholicism at a low ebb, a vital preaching of the Gospel holds a great attraction for these multitudes that have never known assurance of salvation. At the moment there are no closed doors in Latin America.

LITERACY, LINGUISTICS AND LITERATURE

IT HAS BEEN ESTIMATED that at least 50 million adults are learning to read each year. This world-wide drive for literacy highlights two factors of keen interest to mission boards. The first of these is the problem of linguistics. The second is the problem of literature for the new literates to read.

LINGUISTICS

This may be defined as the science of learning a language and reducing it to writing. This task is very important if the Word of God is to be given to people in their own language.

According to the most recent statistics released by the American Bible Society, dated December, 1958, the entire Bible or a portion of it has now been published in 1,136 languages. These are broken down as follows: languages in which the whole Bible has been published, 215; languages in which the complete New Testament has been published, 273; the remainder have at least one Gospel or one whole book of the Bible.

No complete Bible in a new language was published during 1958, but the whole New Testament was published for the first time in three new languages during the last two years, and parts of the Bible were printed for the first time in nine other languages. In addition to these there are 80 or more languages in which short passages of the Bible have been published, but for which no complete book of the Bible has been provided. There is no record available of the number of languages into which translations of the Scriptures are being made at the present time.

The linguistic problem is one that is automatically created for us by the existence of so many languages in the world. *Chambers' Encyclopedia,* 1950 edition, states that there are approximately 3,076 languages in the world, not counting dialects. But since that time more languages have been discovered; for example, in New Guinea. We are informed that in all of New Guinea there are at least 1,200 language groups and that 579 of them are in the Australian section of New Guinea alone. And in all of these 579 languages, only two have the complete Bible, 10 have the complete New Testament, and 30 have portions of the Scriptures. A very modest estimate would indicate that there are at least 2,000 tribes from language groups in which there is no Scripture. These 2,000 tribes have approximately 150 million people in them.

In Brazil, according to the government, there are approximately 3 million Indians speaking 186 languages, plus many dialects. Of these it seems reasonable to believe that not more than 50 are being reached. This leaves 136 that still have to be reached with the Word and have their language reduced to writing. The sad fact was also published that in the last fifty years at least 70 tribes have died out. This means that 70 entire tribes have disappeared from the earth never having heard the Gospel of Jesus Christ.

Speaking of the great needs of Africa, Dr. Albert Helser says that in all of Africa only 340 language groups have the Scriptures and that 500 language groups have nothing. In addition to these 840 languages of Africa there are at least 3,000 dialects. The challenge, therefore, is for linguists. It is estimated that on an average it takes four linguists to reduce a language to writing and initiate the translation of Scriptures. There are training facilities available in the field of linguistics to prepare these 8,000 candidates that would be needed to handle 2,000 languages within the next fifteen years, or sooner if facilities are enlarged. The need is for men and women called to this work and the funds to send them out.

LITERATURE

From the very beginning of modern missions, an effort has been made to take the printed book and the printed page along with the missionary to serve as ammunition. However, in recent years literature has become increasingly important. This is due partially to the existence of the many new literates and the newer methods of teaching people to read, but also to the efforts of non-Christian groups who have made such excellent and beneficial use of literature. The Communists have taught us how to spread doctrine by the printed page. Many of the so-called Christian sects have covered whole towns with their literature. So, evangelicals are gradually awakening to the great opportunity that confronts us in this field.

For a number of years now there have been literature committees within mission ranks, particularly in the older mission organizations. Our main concern is that a flood of literature may go forth from the evangelical mission boards who are now showing a great interest in this matter. Some of the finest mission presses that can be found overseas today are those which have been established by these missions.

To supplement the organizations of many of the older denominations and mission boards, evangelicals have begun to establish their own literature agencies. In the United States the Evangelical Literature Overseas organization is sponsored jointly by the Evangelical Foreign Missions Association and the Interdenominational Foreign Mission Association. This has become their official agency to stimulate interest in literature and to act as a service agency for the literature committees of our many evangelical missions. Part of the function of ELO has been to stimulate the setting up of co-ordinating organizations overseas. The largest of these is Evangelical Literature for Latin America, commonly known as LEAL.

From its headquarters in San Jose, Costa Rica, LEAL reaches out to all of Latin America, mailing out news bulletins and sponsoring conferences in an endeavor to co-ordinate the work of those who are publishing Gospel literature in Spanish. As a direct by-product of this organization a similar one has been established in Brazil for the Portuguese language.

All over the world, a total of 22 literature fellowships have come into being, some of them encouraged by ELO and others springing up as a result of other evangelical co-operation. A good example of the latter is the Evangelical Literature Fellowship of India, which was established by the Evangelical Fellowship of India, an organization including most of the evangelical forces of India. These fellowships in general make surveys of existing literature, endeavor to determine the needs of the various language groups within their area, and endeavor to achieve the greatest possible degree of co-operation and co-ordination. They have also studied new ways of distributing literature, in order to increase the volume being published and distributed.

There are several matters of particular interest in the field of evangelical literature around the world. One is the advent of the popular-type magazine, the first of which was the *African Challenge* published in Nigeria. This magazine, published monthly, and for sale on the newsstands of English-speaking countries throughout Africa, established a pattern and method to guide those interested in similar work in other language groups. Within the last ten years at least five other magazines of this type have appeared in Africa, four of them in the Congo and one in South Africa. Those being published in the Congo are in French and three of the local languages, and the one in South Africa is an English edition. A similar magazine, but slightly different in style, is being printed in Hong Kong for the Chinese. The *Caribbean Challenge* has shown phenomenal growth, reaching at least 60,000 monthly throughout all the English-speaking West Indies. A Spanish-language magazine has been discontinued temporarily. Studies are being made with regard to the possibility of starting similar magazines in several other countries of Asia and the Arabic-speaking world.

A second matter of interest is the great upsurge in correspondence courses. Correspondence courses are not new; they have been used for decades. But in recent years they have been used for two main purposes: (1) the winning of men and women to Christ through a simple Gospel course; (2) the strengthening of new converts through a simple course on the Christian life. An excellent example here is the Light and Life Course, originally written for use in India. This course is now used in all the main languages of India and has been translated into many others, so that at the present time this correspondence course in the Gospel of John is being used in 43 countries and in 41 different languages. One correspondence school in South India has 90,000 active correspondents taking the course. The other type of correspondence course might best be typified by that used by the Radio Station HCJB of Quito, Ecuador. For many years this station has had a Bible Institute of the Air which uses a more advanced correspondence course, sending out textbooks and giving examinations to prepare young men and women as workers in the ministry of Jesus Christ.

In some countries, book clubs and tract clubs have been brought into being, particularly through the instrumentality of these literature fellowships. The book clubs have proved to be a good way of providing inexpensive reading material for national workers, and the tract clubs encourage the writing of new tracts as well as the distribution of existing literature.

The challenge, the possibilities, the needs in this field of literature are almost incomprehensible. There are perhaps five major problems. One, to secure the co-operation of those interested in literature. (Literature specialists do not always see the need of co-ordinating their activities.) Two, to provide the funds necessary to produce vast quantities of literature. (Often those who have a great interest in sending out preachers of the Gospel fail to see the need of supplying them with ammunition.) Three, to provide the mission fields with the right kind of literature. (Surveys reveal a preponderance of literature for the Christian, but often literature for the unsaved is sadly lacking.) Four, to encourage in evangelicals the zeal that is needed to accomplish the task of spreading the written Word. (Perhaps we need some of the fervor shown by the sects who annually distribute millions of pieces of their literature.) Five, to encourage writing by the nationals.

RADIO

WHEN THE PIONEER MISSIONARY RADIO STATION HCJB was founded in Quito, Ecuador, some thirty years ago, few had imagined the immense potential of radio in reaching the world with the Gospel. Today there are 22 missionary radio stations, which with their combined ministry can reach just about every corner of the globe. Any statement of the number of languages being broadcast over these stations would be out of date because new languages are being added constantly. The following map will give some idea of the scope of these stations but this is only part of the story. In every country where it is possible to buy radio time the Gospel is on the air. In Latin America, for example, the Gospel may be broadcast commercially in all the countries except Mexico, Colombia and Paraguay. But, on the other hand, these are hearing the Gospel from stations in adjoining countries.

An interesting factor is that this missionary radio broadcasting effort has been largely the work of strong evangelical missions. Also, a great majority of those operating Gospel broadcasting stations are American organizations. The World Conference on Missionary Radio (headquarters in Talcottville, Connecticut) ties together most of the existing missionary radio stations. This organization publishes the *Foreign Missionary Radio,* as a source of information about the work of these stations.

WORLD MISSIONARY RADIO
STATIONS
April, 1959

1 HCJB—Casilla 691, Quito, Ecuador
2 TIFC—Apartado 2710, San Jose, Costa
    Rica
3 DZAS—Box 2041, Manila, Philippines
4 CP-27—Cajon 8, La Paz, Bolivia
5 HOXO—Apartado 3269, Panama City
6 4VEH—Box 1, Cap Haitien, Haiti
7 TGNA—Apartado 601, Guatemala City,
    Guatemala, C.A.
8 DYSR—Dumaguete City, Philippines
9 KAIM—1136 12th Ave., Honolulu,
    Hawaii
10 ELWA—P.O. Box 192, Monrovia,
    Liberia, West Africa
11 THE VOICE OF TANGIER—Box 2219,
    Tangier, Morocco, N. Africa
12 KSEW—Box 258, Sitka, Alaska
13 HLKY—91 Chong No 2 Ka, Seoul,
    Korea
14 IBRA—Tangier, Morocco, N. Africa
15—WIVV—Box 338, Vieques, Puerto
    Rico, W.I.
16 HLKX—Box 16, Inchon, Korea
17 KSAB—Naha, Okinawa
18 PJA6—Aruba, Netherlands Antilles,
    West Indies
19 4-VI—Cayes, Haiti
20 YNOL—Managua, Nicaragua
21 HLKT—Taegu, Korea

STATIONS BEIN(

(1) KSBU—Okinawa (Far East Broad-
    casting Company)
(2) Nome, Alaska (Arctic Broadcasting
    Ass'n.)
(3) Pusan, Korea (Christian Radio Mis-
    sion)
(4) Tegucigalpa, Honduras (Conservative
    Baptist Home Mission Society)
(5) Salta, Argentina (Conservative Baptist

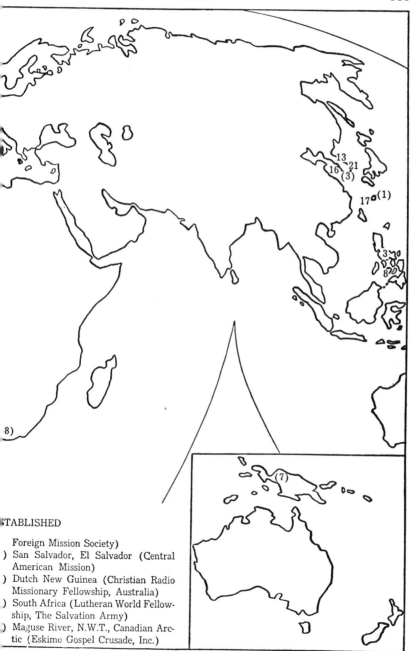

In mission lands where radio stations are not owned by mission boards, a number of recording studios have been established. Here a variety of Gospel programs are prepared and taped. These programs may be broadcast locally over commercial stations or sent to international stations that will beam them back into the country. A number of missions in Japan, India and Formosa co-operate in the preparation of tapes to be released over the powerful radio voice of DZAS in Manila. Many thousands of miles away, others are taping broadcasts and sending them to Radio Station ELWA in Liberia, which transmits them out over most of Africa. The same is true of programs taped in Spanish and sent to Tangier for broadcasting into Spain. Broadcasts in other languages are prepared for other sections of Europe. From Latin America, the Far East and Europe messages beamed to the Communist countries are taking the Gospel to those behind the Iron Curtain.

Radio has a vast potential for arousing interest in literature, particularly in correspondence courses. Sometimes there are phenomenal results. For example, a broadcast in one of the Southeast Asian languages, originating from the Far East, was heard in the heart of Arabia. This broadcast offered a correspondence course. The listener, hearing his own language in the heart of Arabia, wrote to his home in Southeast Asia for the course. Thus, inspired by radio and instructed by mail, this listener is studying the Word of God in the heart of the land of the Muslims.

Two other matters should be mentioned with regard to this great program. 1) The constant effort to establish new stations. We hope that soon there will be new missionary broadcasting stations in Okinawa, Alaska, Korea, Honduras, Argentina, El Salvador, Dutch New Guinea and South Africa. (2) The portable missionary. This is the transistor, pre-tuned radio set, operated on flashlight batteries. Placed in a village home and turned on at prearranged times, these portable missionaries are preaching the Gospel to multitudes who have no other way of hearing it.

RECORDINGS

Associated with radio in missionary thinking are recordings of the Gospel message. This has proved to be an excellent method of reaching both literates and illiterates. It is even possible to make records in unwritten languages. One organization alone has in the last twenty years sent out over 2 million records in 1,904 languages. Hundreds of these go for use in tribes that have no written languages. In its last year of operation it added 67 new languages. More than 375,000 records were sent out during 1958. Often these are played on hand-wound phonographs.

Thus, evangelicals are missing no known method of communicating the Gospel to the lost.

MISSIONS AND ECUMENICS

A NYONE READING RELIGIOUS NEWS these days frequently encounters this word "ecumenical" or "ecumenics." The meaning of the word is very similar to that of "catholic." It means universal, the whole world, or, in its present application, the whole visible church. To state it simply, the purpose of the ecumenical movement is to bring about organizational unity of the many Protestant denominations, organizations, societies and churches.

INTERNATIONAL MISSIONARY COUNCIL

While this is not the oldest interchurch organization in modern times (that honor would go to the World Evangelical Alliance established more than a hundred years ago in England and still in existence), the International Missionary Council, organized after the great missions conference in Edinburgh in 1910, is the largest. This is a noncreedal organization in that it does not have a statement of faith or make any theological demands upon its members. It is composed of national Christian councils of mission boards and churches. These councils are set up in individual countries such as the National Christian Council of India, the National Christian Council of Japan, etc. At the present time it is composed of 11 national councils of missions in sending countries (countries from which missionaries are sent), and 23 national Christian councils on foreign mission fields.

There are some organizations of mission boards and churches on mission fields that are not members of the International Missionary Council but have remained independent; for example, the Kenya Christian Council, the Evangelical Federation of the Cameroons, the Evangelical Federation of French West Africa, and the National Evangelical Council of Peru. Since the meeting of the International Missionary Council in Ghana in 1957, where it was voted to merge the International Missionary Council with the World Council of Churches, the Congo Protestant Council has withdrawn its membership from the International Missionary Council.

This brings us to the World Council of Churches. This great ecumenical organization, established in 1948, is composed of church denominations. Its membership is not by countries but by organized national churches, with something less than a hundred members, 47 of which are on mission fields. Ten of the members are not Protestant churches but belong to the Orthodox and other groups. This means that of the total membership probably around 37 are what are known as the younger or newer churches on the mission field. The World Council of Churches takes in the great bulk of Protestant Christians around the world, but it is surprising how many large Protestant groups on mission fields have not affiliated. The products of evangelical missions around the world have consistently refused to become members of the World Council of Churches which is, to a limited degree, a creedal organization. However, their statement of faith is unsatisfactory to most evangelicals, and with regard to membership they follow an inclusive theological policy. This is proved by the fact that they take in the Greek Orthodox Church, the Coptic Church, etc.

The proposal to merge the International Missionary Council with the World Council of Churches was made some years ago and has finally worked toward a climax at the present time. The missionary arms of those churches presently in the World Council of Churches are all in the International Missionary Council, and without a doubt this latter organization served as the handmaiden to bring the World Council of Churches into existence. However, they have remained organically separate until the present time, even though personnel on their boards may be identical in some cases. It is now proposed, after the necessary steps of ratification have taken place, to hold the official meeting in 1960 or 1961 to merge these two organizations. This will immediately produce some missionary problems.

In a number of countries, when the National Christian Councils were established these were not theological bodies but were set up for the purpose of government relations and government representation, and many evangelical missions, both denominational and nondenominational, joined. In a surprising number of cases these missions still belong to these national Christian councils, especially as there is no theological problem involved. However, when the IMC, which includes many of these national Christian councils, merges with the World Council of Churches it will mean that some missions will probably have to take action in order to preserve their testimony and remain true to their conservative or evangelical theological position. This divisive move on the part of evangelicals is actually forced upon them by the determinate action of the ecumenists, who are convinced that the only way to present a united testimony before the world is to bring all into one great organization.

ECUMENICAL MISSIONS

This brings us to another aspect of ecumenics and that is a term now commonly used, "ecumenical missions." There are many aspects of this movement and we will only endeavor to give the basic concept. In view of the fact that in many mission fields the national churches are now organized and in some cases have become members of the World Council of Churches, their denominational mission boards at home have decided that to be consistent with their policy they must completely free these churches to carry on their own program. For the church to be completely independent and indigenous, it is inconsistent to be sending missionaries into these areas to carry on missionary work. However, in many cases missionaries are still occupying strategic places in schools, institutions, or in other ministries within the church. Therefore, they call these missionaries "fraternal workers," or another term, but not the term "missionary." The home denomination continues to supply financial subsidy, and in some cases increases this subsidy, so there is a tendency to put these so-called indigenous or independent churches back onto a mutual aid program. Evangelical missionary leaders see the possibility of several serious consequences that may come from this move.

In the first place, it is taken for granted that these younger churches are completely capable of carrying on the work of propagating the Gospel and that they have an evangelistic and missionary vision. Unless these churches have a real vision to finish the task of evangelizing their own countries this is not apt to take place, and from current observations it is feared that this is going to be the case in a number of areas.

Second, it would seem that the continuance of financial subsidy is going to be a continually weakening force on these younger churches.

The third result is that the evangelical denominational and nondenominational missions will be the ones that take over the task of entering unoccupied territories, entering the unreached areas of the world, and doing the work of linguistics. It has already been observed that this is what evangelicals are doing. There is perhaps another reason for this, that the older denominations and missions which did such heroic work in the last century and the first part of this century have reached a stage of decline as far as expanded missionary work is concerned. Most of the mission agencies show many less missionaries than they had twenty years ago. Over 80 per cent of the present great advance in missionary endeavor (whether it be pioneer work, specialized work in radio and linguistics, or general missionary work) is due to the efforts of the evangelical mission societies in the sending countries.

A fourth problem in ecumenics arises when distinctive younger churches on the mission field are merged to form one large church, such as the Church of South India. Such mergers seem to produce a definite loss in doctrine, in vision, in evangelism and in spiritual power. All meet at the lower common denominator in doctrine and church practice.

Evangelicals are not insensitive to the need of drawing the younger churches together. However, their motivation is different from that of the ecumenical movement. They, too, believe in preserving a oneness of testimony and faith before the world, but they do not believe that the answer is organizational unity. They do not feel that there is any need of a drive to get unity. They believe that their oneness is by faith in Jesus Christ—by the new birth. There is a necessity, however, of a oneness in fellowship and work. For this purpose, the World Evangelical Fellowship was organized in Holland in 1952. Membership included the already existing organizations of the Evangelical Alliance of Great Britain, the National Association of Evangelicals in the United States, the Evangelical Fellowship of India, and some ten other fellowships scattered about the world. Since that time the total membership of the World Evangelical Fellowship has grown to 23. This movement is exactly as its name indicates. It is not an ecumenical movement in the sense that it is a council of churches or that churches as a whole join. It proposes that in each country evangelicals (churches, mission boards or denominations) get together and form a local fellowship, calling it by any name they wish (an alliance, an association, a fellowship). Then these national organizations would join the world organization. Its main purposes are spiritual—fellowship, co-operation, revival, evangelism and prayer. These national fellowships endeavor to promote co-operation at the national level, such as the formation of literature committees, radio committees, etc.

In some countries, such as Guatemala, Costa Rica, Venezuela, Ecuador and others, the national fellowships are nonrelated and do not belong to anything outside their own country. It is to be hoped that this policy will eventually change, and that these strictly evangelical groups may also be brought together into this world fellowship.

The Baptists have banded together in the Baptist World Alliance. Some Baptist groups will not affiliate with any organization that is not Baptist. There are other denominations which have the same policy. In the United States there are several large evangelical denominations that do not affiliate with any other organization. Possibly in the future these may also be brought into such a fellowship.

In conclusion, may we say that it is the determinate policy of some missions and some denominations to maintain this spirit of isolation, believing that they can best defend the purity of doctrine of the church by remaining isolated. However, on mission fields where Christians are such a small minority anyway it would seem that this policy is doomed to failure. If these organizations do not voluntarily encourage the younger churches to associate with some evangelical agency, these smaller churches will automatically be drawn into the larger, more dominant group of the area for fellowship. Thus, in the end, missions will lose their influence over younger churches.

Evangelicals, therefore, are for fellowship and co-operation as long as it can be done without compromising our stand for the faith once for all delivered to the saints.

BIBLIOGRAPHY

Bible Society Record, June, 1959 edition. New York: American Bible Society

Cosmopolitan World Atlas, 1958 edition. New York: Rand Mc-Nally and Company.

Directory of North American Protestant Foreign Missionary Agencies. New York: Missionary Research Library, 1958.

Directory of Protestant Medical Missions. Arthur W. March, compiler. New York: Missionary Research Library, 1959.

Ethnologue, fifth edition. California: The Wycliffe Bible Translators, Inc., no date.

Foreign Missionary Radio, October, 1958, February, March, April, May, June, 1959 editions. Mrs. H. E. Parsons, editor. New York.

Information Please Almanac, 1959 edition. Dan Golenpaul, editor. New York: The Macmillan Company.

Messages and Findings of the Fifth Annual Conference, Evangelical Literature Overseas (December 10-13, 1956). Wheaton: Evangelical Literature Overseas.

Missions Annual, 1959 edition. J. O. Percy, Ivan Allbutt, Douglas C. Percy, compilers. New York: Interdenominational Foreign Mission Association.

Mission Fields Today. A. J. Dain, editor. London: Inter-Varsity Fellowship, 1956.

Population and Vital Statistics Report, January, 1959 edition. New York: Statistical Office of the United Nations.

Protestant Churches of Asia, The Middle East, Africa, Latin America, and The Pacific Area. New York: Missionary Research Library, 1959.

The World Almanac, 1959 edition. Harry Hansen, editor. New York: New York World-Telegram.

Thiessen, John Caldwell, *A Survey of World Missions.* Chicago: Inter-Varsity Press, 1955.

United Evangelical Action, February, 1959 edition. W. S. Mooneyham, editor. Wheaton, Ill.

World Christian Handbook, 1957 edition. W. J. Bingle and Kenneth Grubb, editors. London: World Dominion Press.

NOTES

NOTES

NOTES

NOTES

NOTES

NOTES